# P-47
# PILOTS
## The Fighter-Bomber Boys

*To Brian with best regards*

*Tom Glenn*

*12/20/14*

Tom Glenn

# PROLOG

In reading this book, in the early part of the 21st century, the reader may be amazed with the military accomplishments our young men and women made against, not one but two nations determined to defeat and occupy the United States of America. Germany had been at war with England, France, Belgium and Poland since September of 1939, and was the most powerful war power in Europe. Japan had been at war with China and England because of England's colonies in Asia. On December 7th, 1941 Japan attacked the United States, without warning, and the following day we were at war with the two greatest military powers on the face of our planet, and we were woefully unprepared to defend ourselves.

Germany's submarines began to sink our ships that were carrying supplies to England, The Japanese were advancing to all parts of the Pacific and winning every battle. At that point America could not defend itself, but our youth could, and soon the entire country was involved in a massive war effort. Our enlistments centers were overflowing with young men volunteering for military service, and soon women were replacing men in large numbers as riveters on assembly lines in aircraft plants, and welders in the ship yards. Everyone was dedicated to winning the war; loosing was not an option, we would win or die trying.

By the middle of 1942 we were winning a few battles and our power was growing. However, there was a desperate shortage of pilots, but with little more than determination the United States Army Air Forces increased the number of pilots, who at the beginning of the war numbered 30,000 to a force of 200,000 by mid-1943 and by wars end there were over 16,000,000 men and women in the armed forces That was the way Americans did things in those days, Tom Brokaw named these citizens of America, "The Greatest Generation", but they too are now passing, as all things must. So it is fitting that books, songs, and other historic memorabilia remain to tell the story of that period of events so crucial in our history which made America the number one world power. That is the purpose of this book

It *is this author's fervent hope that those times will never be repeated. That will be the only true memorial to those who valiantly gave their lives for the American Victory in the greatest man made catastrophe ever seen on planet earth.*

First published in 1998 by MBI Publishing Company, 729 Prospect Avenue, PO Box 1, Osceola, WI  54020-0001 USA.

The information in this book is true and complete to the best of our knowledge. All recommendations are made without any guarantee on the part of the author or Publisher, who also disclaim any liability incurred in connection with the use of this data or specific details.

We recognize that some words, model names, and designations, for example, mentioned herein are the property of the trademark holder. We use them for identification purposes only. This is not an official publication.

MBI Publishing Company books are also available at discounts in bulk quantity for industrial or sales-promotional use. For details write to Special Sales Manager at Motorbooks International Wholesalers & Distributors, 729 Prospect Avenue, PO Box 1, Osceola, WI 54020-0001 USA.

Library of Congress Cataloging-in-Publication Data

Glenn, Tom.
     P-47 pilots : the fighter-bomber boys/ Tom Glenn.
       p.  cm.
     Includes index.
     ISBN 0-7603-0548-X (pbk. : alk. paper)
     1.  World War, 1939-1945--Aerial operations, American. 2.  Thunderbolt (Fighter planes) I.  Title.
     D790.G537    1998           98-14352
     940.54'21--dc21

*On the front cover:* The Republic P-47 Thunderbolt, fully loaded with 500-pound bombs and a belly tank, awaits the signal for takeoff.

*On the back cover:*A P-47 squadron on a taxiway awaiting takeoff. Due to the pilot's limited visibility over the nose, crew chiefs rode along on the wings giving taxi directions until the planes were set for takeoff.

Printed in the United States of America

# CONTENTS

# ACKNOWLEDGMENTS

A work of this nature involves more than just the author. Without the help of the following people this book would not be as complete, nor as accurate. My grateful appreciation to Colonel Charles Queen, M.D., U.S.A.F. Retired, for his generous help in providing me with many of his personal photographs that appear in this book; Lt. Colonel Earl Kielgass, U.S.A.F. Retired, whose excellent memory for details and his recall of the events at Metz, France, was of great help; and Bill Holyfield whose constant encouragement kept me going.

To the pilots of the following fighter groups of the Ninth Air Force who were the Fighter-Bomber Boys, and especially to those who gave their lives heroically for the defense of America: the 36th Fighter Group, 48th Fighter Group, 50th Fighter Group, 354th Fighter Group, 358th Fighter Group, 362nd Fighter Group, 365th Fighter Group, 366th Fighter Group, 367th Fighter Group, 368th Fighter Group, 371st Fighter Group, 373rd Fighter Group, 404th Fighter Group, 405th Fighter Group, and the 406th Fighter Group.

To the P-47 Thunderbolt Pilots Association and the Ninth Air Force Association who keep the legend alive.

And finally, to my wife, Maxine, who changed my longhand scratches on yellow paper, time and time again, into readable manuscript form, and spent hour after hour in research. Without her help, the story of the Fighter-Bomber Boys would have remained only my dream.

# INTRODUCTION

A lthough this book covers the Ninth Air Force World War II fighter-bomber campaign in Europe from April 1944 to the end of the war, to gain the true perspective of this weapon, its development and implementation, we must go back to World War I, when the airplane came into its own as a weapon of war.

Originally aircraft were used to observe enemy troops and installations; the next logical step was to equip them with guns and bombs making them an offensive weapon. Because each side followed the same tactical development, they soon began to shoot at each other, and the use of war planes rapidly became highly specialized. Before the end of the war, three types of war planes emerged: the bomber, the observation plane, and the fighter. The bomber was a multi-crew, multi-engine plane that flew over the enemy at 10,000 feet, unloaded its cargo of bombs, and hoped it hit or came close to the intended target. The observation plane continued to carry out the original mission of the war plane, that is, to observe enemy troops, report their position, and direct artillery fire against them. This type usually was a two-seater with a machine gunner in the rear seat as protection against enemy fighters. The fighter was a single-engine, single-seat plane. It was the fighter pilot's job to shoot down enemy bombers and to protect his own bombers by shooting down enemy fighters that were attacking them. Another primary goal of the fighter was to reduce the number of enemy fighters by seeking out their formations on patrol and engaging in massive one-on-one aerial jousting contests; these were aptly named dogfights.

An overwhelming glamour soon attached itself to the fighter pilot. The superb became aces, the fair to mediocre—statistics; the lucky ones survived, and their stories were told in Hollywood movies.

However, the popularity of the war plane, overwhelmingly accepted by the general public, was bypassed by the American military. According to the army, wars were won by artillery barrages and infantry charges; according to the navy, wars were won by sea battles with battleships. The air arm was part of the U.S. Army Signal Corps and had little support from the high command.

After World War I military appropriations were cut severely, and a disproportionate amount of money went to the U.S. Navy. General Billy Mitchell, a flyer during the war and a military aviation advocate, openly challenged this, stating the next war would be won by air power and that his airplanes could sink navy ships. The navy scoffed; Mitchell persisted, and finally in 1921 a test was set up to settle the issue. Captured ships of the German navy were anchored for the test, and Mitchell's pilots sank them. Another test was scheduled, and Mitchell's planes again sank two obsolete American battleships.

The navy saw this as a personal attack and an invasion of their turf. If ships were to be sunk in a future war, the navy would do the sinking because the sea was navy, and the army had no business involving themselves in naval warfare. You'd think the army high command would have been overjoyed with Mitchell's success, possibly even decorating him. But instead they turned on him, relieved him of command, court-martialed him, reduced him in rank, and expelled him from service for five years. Why this harsh treatment? Because he had committed the unpardonable sin in the military—he had challenged his superiors and proven them wrong. Senior flag rank will not tolerate this; the General's and Admiral's code required the utter annihilation of this upstart junior general, and their combined power wreaked its vengeance. He retaliated by resigning. However, to save some face and placate a few angry and powerful congressmen, the army designated the air arm as a separate unit and created the United States Army Air Corps; it was now 1926.

The army did very little to develop the air corps for the next decade, primarily because the senior and powerful generals were all steeped in the traditional branches of infantry, cavalry, and artillery, and it was those branches that had nurtured them to star rank.

The navy had a different problem, however. It now was an accepted fact that aerial bombs could sink battleships; therefore, the development and control of this new weapon must be under the exclusive control of the U.S. Navy. The next decade was fraught with problems, but success finally came; by the mid-1930s they had developed their plane. It was a single-engine, two-man aircraft that could dive directly on a warship and drop its bombs; they called it a dive-bomber. Tactics were also developed. The pilot, flying at 10,000 feet, would find his target, fly almost directly over it, push over, and dive down at an angle of between 70 and 90 degrees. When he was 3,000 feet above the target, he'd release the bombs and then pull out of the dive. In order to keep the plane from going too fast in the dive and tearing itself to pieces, huge flaps called dive brakes were built under the wings, and the pilot would extend these during his dive. This device would keep the speed of the plane well within its structural integrity of under 200 miles per hour.

By now the army had had a change of heart and was convinced the airplane would play a major role in the next war, but that role would be to support the ground troops as an integral part of a military command. By 1935 this strategy was actively developed at the Air Corps Tactical School, Maxwell Field, Alabama. But the air corps was still part of the army, and senior army generals were ground oriented. As a result, command of air units engaged in close air support of ground troops would be under the control of the army ground commander to the exact same extent as artillery and armored units. Army Air Corps generals refused to accept this, but it really didn't matter because the army had no airplanes for the task or pilots trained in this method of coordinated attack.

Although the Army Air Corps was not impressed with the navy's dive-bomber or its tactics, Germany was. Ernst Udet was a German aviator in World War I and was credited with 62 kills, making him an ace 12 times over. In 1938 he held the rank of lieutenant general in the Luftwaffe.

The U.S. Navy was so proud of their accomplishments in perfecting the dive-bomber as a naval weapon that they eagerly demonstrated it whenever possible. On one such occasion General Udet was one of the observers. He was so impressed that, as the chief of the technical bureau of the German air force, he arranged to buy one. The record is unclear as to the exact aircraft or the number he purchased. It was either a Douglas SBD Dauntless or a Curtis SB2C Helldiver, and it's possible he purchased both.

A civil war was now raging in Spain, and Germany secretly sent its pilots to fly for Francisco Franco's revolutionaries to gain combat experience and test their airplanes. It was now 1937. They learned a great deal about ground support operations, and coupled with their borrowed knowledge of the U.S. Navy dive-bombing airplane and its techniques, developed their Stuka JU87 dive-bomber. When it was introduced it was a two-man plane and had dive brakes. Their original ground support airplane, the HE-51, was a single-seater and did not have dive brakes.

On September 1, 1939, the world was shocked by the fierce onslaught of Germany's armored columns and the relentless dive-bombing by the Stukas. It was called Blitzkrieg—the ultimate coordinated attack of air and ground forces. They defeated Poland in 27 days.

The United States Army now became so concerned about their lack of a ground support aircraft that senior commanders began to demand one based along the lines of the Stuka, but General Arnold, who was then head of the air corps, disagreed with the concept and design of the dive-bomber as an aircraft for the close support of ground troops. Instead, he ordered a twin-engine light bomber, the A-20 Havoc, built by Douglas Aircraft Company for Britain. Amazingly enough, the German high command had had a change of heart at about this same time. They had found that the slow moving JU87 Stuka dive-bombers were only good against undefended targets, so they were developing their next generation dive-bomber, the JU88—a twin-engine light bomber. But the question was still not settled for the U.S. Army.

Senior army commanders pushed for their Stuka-type dive-bomber, and Arnold continued to resist. In early 1941 United States Army Chief of Staff General George C. Marshall ordered General Arnold to acquire a dive-bomber for the Army Air Corps. There was no such plane available nor did the air corps have any in design. However, the P-51 was in production at North American Aviation Company. It was a single-engine fighter being built for the British as a ground support aircraft. The air corps—as required by Marshall—ordered it but had it modified to navy dive-bomber standards with dive brakes and bomb racks and designated it the A-36.

Operation Torch, the Allied invasion of North Africa, commenced on November 8, 1942. Now the concept of close air support to ground troops would be tested by the

United States Army. The results weren't quite a disaster, but they were a long way from successful. The air corps A-36 dive-bomber was a mediocre performer at best.

By now the Battle of Britain was history, and everyone had gained tactical knowledge from it. The British learned it was possible to defend against heavy bombers if you had enough fighters to keep them from reaching their targets. The Americans learned that it would take repeated raids with massive air armadas to halt military production and break the civilian population's will to resist. And the Germans learned that their Stuka dive-bomber had been rendered obsolete by advanced antiaircraft technology. Consequently, the JU87 was withdrawn from combat in Western Europe; it was no longer a first-line weapon.

The British had been fighting in North Africa before the commencement of Operation Torch (invasion of North Africa, November 8, 1942). They had never developed a dive-bomber, but found they could provide very effective air support to ground troops by simply taking a first-line fighter and hanging bombs under its wings and belly. There were obvious advantages to this concept. Fighters were built for speed; therefore a fighter could make a dive-bomb attack without fear of the plane disintegrating from excessive speed. Second, it could take care of itself; if attacked by enemy fighters, it merely jettisoned its bombs and engaged in a dogfight on equal terms, and finally, it negated the requirement of a separate airplane with the added production and maintenance problems that would necessarily entail. In their wisdom they determined that a fighter could be a dive-bomber, but a dive-bomber could never be a fighter. Thus the day of the dive-bomber was over and the fighter-bomber was born.

Everybody got the word except the U.S. Navy, which stubbornly hung to its dive-bomb technique perfected against targets towed on a placid sea in the mid-1930s. When they were later committed to combat, entire squadrons were shot out of the sky without dropping so much as one bomb on the enemy target. However, in defense of navy doctrine, during the Battle of Midway the SBD Dauntless, the navy's first-line dive-bomber, was credited with sinking four Japanese aircraft carriers. The down side was that this was a very short battle lasting less than 24 hours, and, of the 128 dive-bombers sent into battle, 40 were lost. Based on this performance, a Ninth Air Force fighter-bomber group in Europe would only last three days. Putting it another way: every fighter-bomber group would lose one squadron per mission, and in three missions would be totally wiped out.

Another consideration was target size. Diving at an angle of 70 to 90 degrees meant the bombs had to be released at least 3,000 feet above the target in order to have enough altitude to pull out of the dive. Now, that may be okay if you're aiming at an aircraft carrier, but if you're aiming at a tank or heavy artillery piece, you wouldn't even come close. To hit these targets, the pilot had to get in close—very close; the point of release was less than the length of a football field, and you surely couldn't do this in a 70-degree dive.

There would be more than a year between the end of Operation Torch and D-Day—the invasion of Europe. During this time a great deal of energy was spent on how to use this new weapon—the fighter-bomber—to its best advantage.

By unanimous agreement between air and ground commanders, the number-one priority became air superiority. First-line fighter planes would not be committed to a fighter-bomber role until the Allies had achieved total superiority in the skies over Europe. Second, target selection would be on the highest level jointly between field army commanders and tactical air force commanders, and ground control teams would be trained to operate at the front to identify targets for the pilots.

Army commanders finally accepted the fact that they could not command and control groups of fighter-bombers as they controlled brigades of field artillery. This produced a further separation between air corps and ground officers, but enhanced mutual respect for each others' combat role.

There was, however, one serious shortcoming: all the work of refining the fighter-bomber concept and how it was to be used once the invasion of Europe got underway was done at the highest echelon of command. Unfortunately, none of this ever got to the training command; therefore, nothing was done in regard to the actual technique of how to fight—in an airplane—close to the ground—in direct support of ground troops. Once the invasion started it would be on-the-job training for the Fighter-Bomber Boys. It was deadly work. They had to learn fast or die.

# chapter 1

# WINGS

During World War II, prior to D-Day, the world wondered. What would happen when Allied ground troops finally assaulted Fortress Europe? German infantry divisions were waiting; Rommel's Panzers were waiting; supplies and reinforcements were stockpiled, all for the purpose of driving the invasion forces back into the sea. But Eisenhower was ready with a new awesome weapon: the fighter-bomber. An aircraft designed as a fighter but able to carry bombs under its wings and strapped to its belly. A plane that could knock out a Tiger tank, pulverize a reinforced gun emplacement in a single pass; a plane that could dive at 500 miles an hour and drive its bombs deep into concrete bridge abutments, which a few seconds later would explode, collapsing the entire structure.

A weapon of such versatility that German troops by the thousands surrendered after being mercilessly attacked by it from the air, yet never being fired upon by Allied ground forces. They surrendered because they had been defeated by the fighter-bomber.

It came charging out of the blue into the heat of battle like the cavalry of old, arriving just in time to save the dog-face or the tanks that were about to be overrun by German forces.

What was this fearsome flying beast, the thing the German ground troops called the Jabo? It was the P-47 Thunderbolt, the largest and most deadly one-man airplane in World War II—but it didn't fly itself.

This is the story of the pilots who flew the P-47 Thunderbolt fighter-bomber. They lived in the mud, ate out of mess kits, wore G.I. boots, and flew out of postage stamp-sized airfields a few minutes flying time from the front lines. They were far removed from the glamour of dogfights and air-to-air combat, where the enemy was another plane, not a human being. The fighter-bomber pilot was a killer. He saw his bullets tear bodies apart; he saw his bombs explode in the middle of gun emplacements, shredding gun, ammunition, and German soldiers into small bits. He shot it out with antiaircraft guns, tanks, and armored cars at point-blank range. In most cases these encounters were not over until one or the other was dead. Victory was living to fly another day; defeat was death.

# CHAPTER 1: WINGS

They were not glamorized. Hollywood made no movies about them, and no book, up to now, has ever told their story. Yet they turned the tide in many a battle, saved countless soldiers from certain death, and were in command of one of the most powerful weapons used in the ground war.

To understand their story, you must go back a half century to the early days of war planes, and you must understand what patriotism meant then, why young men, the cream of the nation, were willing to give up their lives to defend America. That was not just an idle expression—they did it.

The cadet pilots came from every state in the union. The training was fierce, the washout rate high, but if they succeeded, they won that coveted prize—a pair of silver wings. A select few of the newly commissioned pilots were then introduced to the P-47 Thunderbolt, but more training was needed.

By today's standards the World War II P-47 Thunderbolt was crude and unsophisticated. There was no pressurized cockpit, no ejection seat, no electronic controls, no radar or guidance system, no computer, no heads-up display, and no lock-on targeting system. It had a stick and rudders that were controlled by muscle power. The pilot wore no G-suit, no bulletproof clothing; the cockpit environment was hostile, and a simple ring and bead gun sight was all he had to get him on the target.

To be successful with at least a reasonable chance of surviving, the pilot had to have complete mastery of his airplane, for once he went into battle there was no time to concentrate on flying—that had to be instinctive. He must focus on the target, and even though it was heavily defended, he must press his attack and let nothing deter him from closing to point-blank range before firing or releasing his bombs.

If he lived long enough, he became an element leader and then a flight leader. These positions came with added responsibility—added responsibility to destroy his assigned target and added responsibility for the survival of the pilots under his command. Training days were over, combat was the Big Time. Being a hot pilot, however, did not guarantee survival, but the opposite guaranteed a listing on the casualty report.

There were less than 3,000 of these gallant young men living under extremely difficult circumstances, yet they performed impossible feats of daring and courage. *P-47: The Fighter-Bomber Boys* is their story, an excellent account of a hitherto untold part of World War II that has great historical importance.

I was fortunate to be one of the fighter-bomber boys, and this story is about us and our beloved Thunderbolt. I do not mean to imply that we won the war all by ourselves or that the war would have been lost without our participation—that would be the height of egotistical stupidity. Nor do I intend to imply that we had the roughest combat duty in the war—again that would be idiotic. It is not my intention to demean other fighting units, other aircraft, branches of the service, or even other theaters of operations. I certainly don't mean to slight the British and Canadian Air Forces and the excellent air-ground support they gave to their own troops.

But this story is about one particular airplane, the P-47 Thunderbolt, and about the pilots who flew it in the Ninth Air Force on air-ground missions beginning prior to D-Day and ceasing on the last day of the war. It is a faithful account from my records, from conversations with many other Thunderbolt pilots, and from research at the Air Force Historical Records section, Maxwell Air Force Base, Montgomery, Alabama.

War in the air holds a fascination unequaled by any other area of combat. Regardless of the geographical location, the particular war, or the people engaged in it, the winged warrior is unique. He ascends to the ultimate—the knight in shining armor. His only peers are other air warriors, yet within this sacrosanct fraternity there are divisions: the fighter pilot, the bomber pilot, and one who does both—the Fighter-Bomber Boy.

War is the business of killing, and killing is what the fighter-bomber pilot was supposed to do. Bomber pilots flew five miles high over the enemy target, the bombardier released the bombs, and nobody on board actually saw those bombs kill a human being. Fighter pilots shot down enemy fighters—that was their target—the enemy fighter plane. The fighter-bomber pilot had a different role to play. His job was to kill German soldiers. He killed them in their tanks, their half tracks, their staff cars, at their guns, and in open fields.

This story, then, is not about aerial combat five miles in the sky; it's about using an airplane to fight at tree-top level, where the face of the enemy was clearly visible.

With few exceptions I have purposely not identified individuals by name or unit. To do so may bring grief to family survivors of the pilots involved. In some cases it could bring embarrassment because even we sometimes broke the code of honor. Further, this is not about a particular fighter-bomber pilot, or group, or squadron. There were 15 groups of fighter-bombers in the Ninth Air Force flying the famed P-47 Thunderbolt. Most did the same type of work.

If you interject present day values into this story, you will be the loser. The historical perspective must remain. Our country was viciously and cowardly attacked by Japan. Germany subsequently declared war on us. We were defending our way of life. From all parts of the nation came young men who loved their country and were willing to fight and, if necessary, die for it. They trained as pilots, learned to fly, and then to kill, even though killing was totally contrary to their normal values.

So come along with me, sit through some briefings, fly a few missions, get drunk with us, go on leave where the primary target is sex, and dodge a few buzz bombs in London.

# chapter 2
# THE AIRPLANE

In this day and age, "Fighter-Bombers" are a standard part of the U.S. arsenal—but it was not always so. The term, "Fighter-Bomber," used during World War II, was not an official title; there was no airplane designed as a fighter-bomber. The name was coined to identify aircraft used for air-ground support missions because that work combined dropping bombs, a job normally done by bombers, and aerial combat plus strafing, a job normally done by fighters. Hence, when one plane was able to do both, it became a fighter-bomber.

The most effective plane for this role was the P-47 Thunderbolt. It is ironic that it was originally designed as a high-altitude escort fighter but actually became the most successful air-ground support aircraft of World War II. When the Eighth Air Force began the daylight bombing of Hitler's Europe, it soon became evident that a first-line fighter was needed to escort the B-17s to their targets and return. There was one additional problem: this new escort plane had to be capable of fighting at 30,000 feet. At that time no airplane in existence could accomplish that. The decision was made to give that task to Republic Aviation; they were the builders of the P-47 Thunderbolt, and just maybe it could be beefed up to do the job.

They did it by using a more powerful engine and adding a turbo-supercharger. The supercharger supplied pressure to the engine at high altitude to compensate for the lower atmospheric pressure that existed there. This meant the engine could not only operate, but operate with power and performance six miles above the earth. Soon the Thunderbolts were on their way to England and filling the squadrons of the Eighth Fighter Command. True to its design requirements, it could out-fight the best the Luftwaffe had to offer. Its record was exemplary: the P-47 Thunderbolt shot down more German planes than any other aircraft in the U.S. Army Air Corps—but it had one serious shortcoming. The Thunderbolt, with its huge, powerful engine, was a gas hog. It used 100 gallons of high-octane gasoline an hour in normal cruise; while engaged in combat, it could use up to 400 gallons an hour. This meant that as the Eighth Air Force B-17s penetrated deeper into Germany, the P-47s couldn't stay with them all the way to the target. To overcome this problem, wing tanks and belly tanks were added, but the Luftwaffe immediately countered by changing their tactics. Now the German fighters attacked the bombers as they first crossed into their territory. The Thunderbolts had to jettison their external tanks in order to fight; however, once their tanks were dropped the German pilots would often break off the attack, but they had accomplished their mission—the Thunderbolts would not be able to stay with the bombers all the way to the target and return. The Luftwaffe would simply wait. Soon the Thunderbolts would have to leave the bombers and return to England due to their diminishing fuel supply. Now the bombers were meat on the table for the Luftwaffe, and the losses were staggering. Thus, there existed a perfect example of the axiom of military power and strategy: for every weapon there is a counter-weapon; for every tactic there is a counter-tactic; the winner is the one who uses the right combination at the right time.

The lack of fighter cover to the target and return was the major cause of the tremendous losses in heavy bombers sustained by the Eighth Air Force. But that was soon to change; there was an airplane being redesigned to fulfill this need. It was the P-51 Mustang. Originally designed at the request of England as a low-flying plane for dive-bombing and strafing, it was now redesigned as a high-altitude bomber-escort fighter. Its original Allison inline engine was replaced with the Rolls Royce Merlin engine; the fuel capacity increased, and with slight aerodynamic changes to its underbelly, it was a match for the Thunderbolt, but it had one overriding improvement: it could go the distance. True, it had less firepower, only six machine guns compared to the Thunderbolt's eight, but its stingy fuel consumption of only 65 gallons an hour made it a true long-distance escort fighter.

Although the P-51 never attained the kill rate of the Thunderbolt, it eclipsed the Thunderbolt's role as an escort fighter. By early 1944, P-51s were the escort fighter of choice by the Eighth Air Force, and it gained its fame by defeating the Luftwaffe at every encounter. Truly, America now ruled the skies of Europe.

But the Thunderbolt still had an important role to play. Prior to D-Day, both P-51s and P-47s went on low-level missions bombing and strafing enemy installations. It became evident that the P-51, even though it was originally designed for this purpose, was not up to the task. True, it handled well close to the ground, but it had one glaring defect for this type of warfare: Its liquid-cooled inline engine proved too vulnerable to ground fire. The smallest hit in any part of the cooling system would soon disable the engine as the coolant would be expelled through its wound, and the engine would seize from overheating.

This was not a problem with the Thunderbolt. Its huge air-cooled, twin-row radial engine could still operate with cylinders actually shot away, and the engine provided some protection for the pilot in frontal attacks. There were other differences: the Thunderbolt had one-third more firepower than the Mustang; it could outdive any airplane in the world; and even though it was designed as a high-altitude fighter and originally restricted in low-altitude operations, with a little coaxing and a lot of respect and tender loving care, it performed marvelously at tree-top level.

So, all things considered, the Mustang became the high-altitude escort fighter and was rarely used for ground attack, and the Thunderbolt became the air-ground support plane and again gained fame, but this time as the best fighter-bomber of World War II. Thus, the two best fighter aircraft flown in the European theater attained their greatest glory—not in their original design role—but in the direct opposite; makes you wonder how we won the war.

# chapter 3

# THE PILOT

Bomber pilots flew with a crew of several other airmen. There was a copilot, navigator, bombardier, and several gunners. The P-47 was a single-place airplane. The lone pilot did it all: he flew, navigated, shot the guns, and dropped the bombs. It's a one-man show but done as a team effort. The squadron is the team, and each member, even though he attacks the target on his own, is a member of the team. There's no room for the individual hot dog, picking targets of his choosing and fighting the war the way he sees it. Teamwork is essential to success and survival, but so is individualism. So the qualities necessary to become a good fighter-bomber pilot were many and varied.

At a recent reunion of the Western P-47 Thunderbolt Pilots Society in Las Vegas, several of us were sitting in the hospitality room sipping drinks and reminiscing about our flying days. Each pilot present had flown a minimum of 50 missions.

"Tell me," I began, "what characteristics were absolutely necessary to become a good fighter-bomber pilot?"

"You had to be nuts," someone said. "How about stupid," someone else added, and everyone laughed.

"I'm serious, you guys—give me your best assessment; it's for a good cause."

"Well, I would say," one guy began, "you had to be an exceptionally good pilot, have plenty of guts, and damn quick reactions."

"Aggressive," the next one added. "You had to be aggressive. In my squadron we had a policy—the first flak gun that opened up on us at the target was immediately attacked by a full flight. And you'd be surprised how many times the rest of their gunners just didn't shoot—they didn't wanta tangle with us."

The only pipe smoker among us took a big puff and drifted a cloud of blue smoke over the table. "Tell you what I think," he began. "You had to be cocky, conceited, self-confident, and believe you were the best in the squadron, and that you'd survive. Yeah, an' above average survival instinct." There was general agreement on this.

One of the guys had stayed in the Air Force and retired as a bird colonel. He took a sip from his drink, put his glass on the table, and said, "There's one thing nobody's mentioned," he began. "I had some friends that flew 17s [B-17s] with the Eighth. They told me they never saw their bombs hit anything—they just flew the airplane—the bombardier dropped the bombs, so as far as they were concerned they didn't personally kill anyone. You get what I mean? We killed! That's a big difference. You didn't have to enjoy it, but you had to do it at close quarters, just like the infantry guys we supported."

In addition to these qualifications as expressed by the pilots who'd been there, the fighter-bomber pilot had to be able to get along with the members of his team, like and be liked by his fellow squadron members, and be able to teach new pilots the tricks of the trade. It also helped if he knew engines and the other mechanical aspects of his plane. He should be able to troubleshoot problems in the air and nurse a sick or wounded plane home.

It would be expecting too much to find all of these characteristics in every P-47 fighter-bomber pilot who flew in Europe; however, the more of those attributes he had, the better his chances of living, and what were his chances of living?

While doing research for this book, I found that no official record exists by squadron or group of the fighter-bomber pilots in the Ninth Air Force who were killed in action during the European campaign. To honor those of my group, on the 50th anniversary of the end of the war in Europe, we held a commemorative memorial service. By comparing memories, log books, and examining the records of all American cemeteries in Europe, we found that my squadron had lost 44 pilots. This did not count any killed in accidents or any form of training flights; these were all killed by direct enemy action on combat missions. When you consider that the squadron averaged about 30 to 35 pilots at any given time, it gives an idea of the price paid by the Fighter-Bomber Boys.

But pilots, ready and eager for combat, were not made overnight. The total time from raw civilian to assignment with a combat squadron was about a year and a half. Fighter and fighter-bomber pilots were extremely conceited; they considered themselves the elite of the flying fraternity, and well they should. Less than one out of a hundred of the cadet graduates achieved the status of combat fighter, or fighter-bomber pilot.

The selection process started in preflight. Prior to that you had to be appointed by the Aviation Cadet Board. There were physical examinations in each phase of this pre-aviation cadet program. Then it was off to the aviation cadet center where about two weeks were spent undergoing extensive physical examinations, a battery of academic tests, interviews with psychiatrists, and psychological testing. They stuck you in the finger for blood, in the arm for more blood; you peed in a bottle; they looked up your rear end and examined what hung between your legs. You put square pegs in square spaces and round ones in round spaces. They asked you if you ever drank, got drunk, masturbated, were a virgin, or smoked, and above all, why you wanted to be a pilot.

Based on the results of these tests, if you passed all of them, you were appointed an aviation cadet. Cadet pilots were sent to four different schools: Preflight, Primary, Basic, and Advanced. Each school was a nine-week course. Preflight consisted of academic work in the aviation and military field. There was no flying but plenty of calisthenics, running, marching, and a full dress parade once a week. After Preflight came Primary school where half the day was devoted to academic work and the other half to flight training; in between, the physical conditioning program continued. This was where you "soloed." Primary had the highest washout rate other than the initial selection process. Only about half the class could expect to go on to further training.

Basic flight school was next. The airplane was bigger and faster, with more technological advancements such as flaps, propeller pitch control, and a two-way radio. By the end of Basic the cadet had experienced night flying, formation, cross country navigation, and some instrument flying. Academic work and physical conditioning continued.

At the completion of Basic the selection process again intervened to determine which cadets would continue training as single-engine pilots and which would train in multi-engine. If you were hot, aggressive, self-sufficient, and super eager, you had a good chance at single-engine which led to that coveted goal—the fighter pilot.

Advanced flight school for single-engine cadets was the proving ground. In nine weeks, if you mastered the AT-6 (advanced trainer built by North American Aviation Co.), got a fairly decent score on the aerial and ground gunnery range, maintained your academic standing, and developed some skills in formation and instrument flying, you would receive your pilot's "Wings" and a commission as a 2nd lieutenant. If you impressed your instructor with your flying abilities and convinced him you had the killer instinct, you'd go on to fighter school, but in fighter school you were no longer a cadet; you were now a rated pilot and an officer in the U.S. Army Air Corps.

For me, fighter school was at Dover Air Base, Dover, Delaware, one of about 10 such schools on the East Coast. It was there that I first met the P-47 Thunderbolt. It took two months to master this beast—at least it seemed like a beast at first—but once I learned its likes and dislikes it behaved like an overgrown pussycat, but I never forgot that a tiger was just under the skin.

Fighter school was called R.T.U.—Replacement Training Unit. You knew you were going over to replace someone who had preceded you, but you always figured your luck would be better than his. The selection process was still at work. Instructors evaluated your competence, and on a regular basis pilots would leave the fighter replacement training squadron to be reassigned to other flying duties. Only the cream remained.

But the fighter pilot role had been changed by the pending ground war in Europe. There was still a need for the traditional fighter pilot; one who fights enemy fighters and bombers in the air, but the invasion of Europe would require pilots who would fight enemy infantrymen, tanks, and armor near the ground. The latter is the fighter-bomber pilot.

At Shrewsbury, England, there was a reception center for all replacement fighter pilots arriving from the United States. Here, they were assigned to combat groups of the Eighth and Ninth Air Force. There were about 200 in my shipment of replacements. Both the Eighth and Ninth Air Force were in need; 35 went to the Eighth; the rest of us went to the Ninth. The high replacement demands of the Ninth Air Force were not lost on us. We had just been made fighter-bomber pilots.

# chapter 4
# THE ORGANIZATION

The Ninth Air Force was the tactical air force, its mission closely related to the day-to-day fighting. There were three tactical air commands in the Ninth Air Force: the Ninth, Nineteenth, and Twenty-Ninth. To prevent confusion, roman numerals were used for their designations (IX, XIX, XXIX). Each fighter-bomber group was assigned to one of these tactical air commands. During the course of the war fighter-bomber groups would be transferred from one tactical air command to another depending on the overall strategy, progress of the war, and where they were needed most. A numbered tactical air command supported a numbered army. Example: the XIX Tactical Air Command (T.A.C.) supported General Patton's Third Army, the IX T.A.C. supported General Hodges' First Army, and the XXIX T.A.C. supported General Simpson's Ninth Army.

A fighter-bomber pilot coming from the replacement pilot pool was assigned to a Group; that was his parent organization. Within that Group he was further assigned to a Squadron; that was his secondary organization. There were three separate squadrons in each group. The total complement of the organization, including the Group Headquarters, was about 850 officers and men.

Each squadron had approximately 35 plus pilots and 25 planes, and it required about 225 people to keep both pilots and planes in top condition and ready for action.

When the squadron was in the air, it encompassed three flights of four planes each. Thus a squadron mission involved 12 planes and a group mission 36. Prior to D-Day, most missions were group missions, and typically the targets were bridges, marshaling yards, troop concentrations, German airfields, armored depots, and rail terminals. These missions were flown from fields in England, which meant crossing the English Channel to get to the targets and crossing again to get back home. Each pilot, in addition to his parachute, wore a Mae West life preserver and sat on a one-man dingy that was attached to his parachute harness. In the event he went down over the channel these devices were supposed to save his life—and indeed they did—but only some of the time.

The English had been at this game of channel crossing since the beginning of the war and had developed an excellent air-sea rescue system. Fortunately, when the

American Air Force started flying, the United States didn't try to duplicate it—they left it to the British. There was one V.H.F. radio channel reserved for air-sea rescue, and each P-47 fighter-bomber was equipped with this radio channel. Using a combination of radar, amphibious airplanes, and high-speed boats, the air-sea rescue service did an outstanding job.

Because of the water temperature of the English Channel, the chances of survival began to diminish rapidly after 10 minutes and hit zero at about a half hour. The one-man life raft extended that time, and if the pilot wasn't injured too badly and could get himself into the raft, he had a pretty fair chance of rescue.

Most of us had an uneasy feeling while crossing over the channel. Looking down from 20,000 feet it was an inhospitable-looking son-of-a-bitch, and half the time, because of weather, you couldn't see it anyway, but you knew it was there. Coming home with battle damage was the worst of nightmares. You could sit there and pray, making all kinds of promises to God to be a good boy from then on if He'd just save your ass this once, or you could curse the Germans for hitting you, or you could look down and say, "You're not going to get me. I'm going to make it home." But just to be on the safe side, you were in contact with those wonderful Brits of the air-sea rescue service. They were just another organization with a single purpose— to save a downed flyer from a watery death so that he could fly and fight again.

After D-Day, when the infantry had taken some real estate away from the Germans, small airfields were constructed, and the fighter-bombers were moved to France. This occurred in the latter part of June, July, and early August of 1944. These were temporary fields—only intended to last for a few weeks. The runways were tar paper layered over dirt and were dangerously short. The flying conditions were not good; the living conditions were not good; the food was not good. But what was GOOD was the English Channel; we didn't have to cross it on our way to and from the battle. The invasion was now in high gear, and the ground troops needed lots of help, so the nature of the missions changed. Few targets warranted a Group attack (36 planes). Most were machine gun nests, a column of Tiger tanks, or a fortified gun position that had an infantry unit pinned down. A squadron of fighter-bombers could clear these obstacles in a matter of seconds. So squadron missions became the order of the day.

Even though the squadron was the secondary assignment, it was the hub of activity and the center of life. All pilots in a given squadron lived together, ate together, flew together, got drunk together, and mourned their missing together. Close bonds were formed that would last a lifetime, even though that lifetime might be only a few weeks.

Within the squadron each pilot was assigned to a flight. Under ideal conditions the squadron had 36 pilots. It took three flights of four planes and pilots to get the squadron into the air. With 36 pilots available, that meant each pilot would fly every third mission, so about every two weeks, or so, he got a three-day pass—at least that's the way it worked while we were flying from England.

The squadron was a self-sufficient organization. It had its own mess, supply, chaplain, doctor, and dispensary. It maintained its own vehicles, disciplined its own troublemakers, and ran its own post office. It had photographers, artists, stenographers (male of course), mechanics, and aircraft and armament repair men of all descriptions. It had its own insignia—usually a tiger clawing something or Mickey Mouse firing machine guns while he rode a bomb to the target.

The pilots were king of the mountain. They had their special mess where they allowed the nonflying officers of the squadron to join them for meals. However, the ground pounders, as they were called, usually gathered at the same table unless they were specifically invited to join a group of pilots. However, this unspoken ostracism did not apply to the flight surgeon, who was the squadron doctor but in actuality was there to ensure the continued good health of the pilots. The flight surgeon walked a thin line. He was loved and hated by the pilots, loved because he could heal them and keep them flying, hated because he could ground them if he suspected any physical or mental deterioration. Thus this entire organization existed for one purpose: to put 12 fighter-bomber pilots and their airplanes into the air. From then on it was up to them to fly through the flak, get to the target, attack it—destroy it—and get back so they could fly again.

The pilots had little to do with anyone but other pilots. They didn't get to know the enlisted men and rarely became friends with the ground pounders. There was, however, one big exception to this—the crew chief. Each pilot, if he lived long enough, got his very own airplane and crew chief. It was the crew chief's responsibility to see that his airplane was in top shape. He knew every nut and bolt in it, all its idiosyncrasies, and woe be to any son of a bitch who hurt it—except the pilot on a combat mission. The crew chief thought of that airplane as HIS airplane; he would loan it to the pilot to fly, but it really belonged to him. He would mourn the pilot if he didn't return, but I always suspected that he missed the plane more.

Pilots, if they had any sense, kept their crew chief happy and that meant booze. The enlisted men had no opportunity to get anything but local rotgut and occasionally some beer from squadron supply. The pilots, however, received a combat ration of whiskey. It was supposed to be two ounces a mission. (That was after you got back.) It was under the control of the flight surgeon, and usually he didn't count too closely, and the pilot could save his ration until he had a goodly amount. The supreme compliment a pilot could bestow on his crew chief was to give him his combat whiskey ration. This had a multi-purpose effect. It proved to the crew chief that the pilot valued his services to the point that he would give up his hard-earned booze to him. It made the crew chief look big in the eyes of his fellow enlisted men because that was a public announcement that his pilot cared for him and respected him. It upset the engineering officer who had administrative control over all the enlisted ground crews; he was not happy seeing an enlisted man enjoy a good drunk on some good whiskey, but he didn't dare come between a pilot and his crew chief, and it didn't really hurt the pilot because he could get all the booze he wanted anyway. Sometimes it was free; occasionally he had to buy it, but it was cheap, and fighter-bomber pilots saw no merit in saving for their old age.

Now all this sounds real good; a smoothly functioning organization, airplanes always repaired, pilots only flying every third mission, a special mess, plenty of booze, and a three-day pass every couple of weeks. I said that's the way it was supposed to be—that's the way it was in England—but after D-Day, when the ground war really got started, we moved to France, and everything changed.

The airfields were dangerously short. The quarters were tents with mud floors; the special pilots' mess didn't exist, nor did plenty of airplanes, flying every third mission, or a three-day leave.

Because these fields were temporary, luxuries were simply not included. Another factor that compounded the problem was combat casualties. They must have been considerably higher than the high command anticipated because the flow of replacement airplanes and pilots didn't keep up with the losses. With fewer pilots left to fly, it meant flying every other mission with little relief from combat flying.

In order to have a good fighting unit, morale must be kept at a high level. With lousy living conditions, meals out of a mess kit sitting in the mud, and no time off, morale was bound to suffer, and it did, but there was a factor introduced that changed the equation. It was the Infantry Liaison Officer assigned to the fighter-bomber squadrons. It was the job of this officer to present the infantry's side of the picture to the fighter-bomber pilots. He was the one who would place his pointer on the map during the mission briefing and say, "Gentlemen, there are troops pinned down at this point. They have wounded and dead, and they're taking more casualties by the hour. They're running short of ammunition because they're cut off by a German Panzer unit that's systematically turning them into dog meat." The fighter-bomber pilot was presented with this scenario on a daily basis and as a result became inextricably linked with that dog face at the front. The fact that he no longer had his officers club seemed insignificant. So morale suffered to some extent but was offset by the fact that the fighter-bomber pilot was still the hero; he could come riding in on his wings of fire and, at the last split second, save his brothers-in-arms. That fact alone was enough of a boost to his ego to offset a serious drop in morale.

On the surface the squadron pilots were a close-knit fraternity. But as with any group, there were inner cliques. If you're talking about 20 to 40 people, naturally everyone isn't going to love everyone else. Now let's take that group and place them in a very unnatural situation, a situation where they are going out daily or every few days for the express purpose of killing people, and as a result, some of them will be killed in the effort. Let's say the flight leader stays a little too long over the target, and as a result your buddy, who was flying his wing, was shot down. You hold him responsible for your buddy's death. You think he is a lousy flight leader. Now let's look at another scenario. The squadron is dive-bombing a reinforced heavy artillery gun emplacement. It's an important target and must be knocked out. The first flight goes in and misses; the second flight goes in, and the flight leader misses but his wing man scores a direct hit. The flight leader claims the hit for himself, and his buddy—one of the other flight leaders—confirms it. The wing man now realizes his flight leader is a less than honorable officer. Other wing men on that mission also realize this is not right, but there is nothing they can do about it. Wing men are 2nd lieutenants and pretty close to being an expendable commodity. So the seeds of dissent are born. After several such incidents there is an undercurrent of dissension within the squadron. It rarely affects their ability in the air, but it's decidedly noticeable on the ground. You don't have to drink with someone who cheated you out of your rightful scores on today's mission.

The "Good Old Boy" syndrome was alive and well in squadrons that had been in existence before the war, or for that matter, any squadron that had been together for any length of time before they went into combat.

Let's say the squadron had trained together in the States before going overseas and into combat. Some pretty close ties were formed during that time. Oddballs or mediocre pilots were weeded out; the ones left were good. The system of rank prevailing in the squadron also extended to the wives. Captains' wives associated with captains' wives, and lieutenants' wives associated with lieutenants' wives, yet all of these people became an extended family. The stress of combat was missing and so were the grudges formed because of it.

Once combat flying started, pilots got killed, and replacements had to be brought in. The replacements were the "New Boys," and the "Old Boys" just couldn't quite accept them as part of their original extended family. The Old Boys also had the rank and seniority, so the New Boys were consciously or unconsciously discriminated against. Their only defense was to join together. As each new replacement pilot arrived, it was the other replacements who welcomed him to the squadron and their cliques. This Old Boy syndrome fostered animosity among the pilots to the point where some actually hated each others' guts and, if possible, never flew together on the same mission.

Once the wheels were up and the squadron assembled and headed for the target, all personal grudges had to cease. A squadron in the air wasn't just 12 airplanes. It was a combination of squadron commander, flight leaders, element leaders, and wing men. It widened out in heavy flak; it drew close in for the bomb run; there were 24 eyes looking out for every airplane, providing immediate help for anyone in trouble. It was a team with a team spirit. The mission objective transcended everything. There was a disciplined single purpose—attack and destroy the assigned target.

# chapter 5

# GOING TO WAR

We received our orders at the pilot replacement pool in Shrewsbury, England, and had two days to get to our new assignment. Four of us drew the same combat group in the Ninth Air Force. We had trained together in the Thunderbolt at Dover Army Air Base, Dover, Delaware, but three of us had been together from our first days as aviation cadets.

It was only a one-day trip to our new station, so we had a day in London to play. London was great in spite of the buzz bombs. We were introduced to this new awesome weapon within a couple of hours of our arrival; one blew the wall out of a pub just minutes before we got there.

We picked up some civilian girls, and after buying them food and booze they seemed eager for an all-night affair. We were elated at our easy conquest until they told us it would be £5 each, about $20 in American money. That was a hell of a shock to our ego. We had latched onto hookers; they were called Piccadilly Commandos. Somehow the thought of buying it just didn't seem right. Here we were practically combat pilots ready to give our all for English ladyfair, and they wanted to sell it. With us it was a question of principle; with them it was a matter of economics, so we parted company and were very disappointed that we'd struck out on our first try in London.

I said we picked them up; actually our meeting was under rather extraordinary circumstances. We had been introduced to the buzz bomb an hour or so before, or at least the devastation caused by one. Now we were wandering around Piccadilly Square looking for women and certainly not thinking of buzz bombs. Suddenly we were aware of a very strange noise. It wasn't an airplane; at least no airplane we had ever heard. The noise grew louder and louder, and we searched the sky for its source, but the cloud cover was down to 400 feet and visibility not much better. We moved out into the street and kept scanning the sky hoping to see something. By now the noise was really loud, and we could actually feel a vibration. Suddenly the noise stopped; we figured whatever it was went away. Then, all at once I was hit from the side, and someone was yelling and pushing me toward a building. In a matter of seconds I was flat on my face along with five other people, all of us piled up in the doorway of a building. Before I could react there was a tremendous explosion.

"What the hell was that," I yelled. "A doodlebug," one of the girls said. We still didn't get it. "A buzz bomb," one of the other girls said. By now we were beginning to get up and brush ourselves off. One of the girls was actually angry. "You dumb Yanks, you could have been killed; didn't you hear it coming?"

"Hell yes, we heard something but couldn't see anything. When it quit, we figured whatever it was was gone." By now we were beginning to realize that we had been in danger.

"Listen, Yank, when the motor stops, it goes into a steep dive. If you hear the motor quit it's very, very close. We figured you were too dumb to know the difference, and when we saw you standing out in the street, we just had to run out and get you."

Actually this was a very heroic thing they did; they left their own shelter, ran out into the open, put a flying tackle on us, and pulled us into the protection of a recessed doorway. When we explained we had just arrived in London a couple of hours ago and didn't know a buzz bomb from a pig's ass, they laughed and forgave our stupidity. We, of course, felt very grateful and suggested drinks and dinner, hoping, of course, that it would lead to better things later. That night when we were going to bed alone and horny, we all agreed our judgment had been flawed in refusing to engage in what was a time honored exchange of personal property.

In that alpha state, that twilight zone between wake and sleep, I came to the sudden realization that I was finally in the war. An enemy soldier actually tried to kill me today; he doesn't know me from Adam, but he shot a robot bomb, hoping to blow someone's head off—maybe mine. So the first shot in anger had been fired, and I'd been on the receiving end. Tomorrow we'd go to our combat squadrons, and soon after that the equation would change. And before I kicked myself again for not taking that girl up on her proposition, I was asleep.

We arrived at our new base about 1100 hours the next day.

"Jesus Christ, what the hell is this!" We had just had our first look at our new home.

"Shit, this is no air base. It's a fucking bivouac with airplanes, no buildings, no runways—nothin'. Glenn, God damn it, you said we'd be living in a castle."

"No, I didn't," I replied. "I said a semi-castle, because that captain instructor at Dover told me we would be living in a semi-castle. Besides—that movie—*A Guy Named Joe*—those guys were living in a semi-castle."

"They were bomber pilots for Christ's sake."

"Well, fighter pilots are better than bomber pilots."

"Maybe we think so, but whoever supplies the castles doesn't think so—besides it was just a movie."

The driver got our stuff out of the truck and dumped it on the ground. "This is group headquarters. You're supposed to check in here." Then he hopped in his truck and drove away.

We were left standing there in class A uniforms, gabardine trench coats, white silk scarves, and jodhpurs that were fast succumbing to mud oozing over their highly polished surface.

One of the guys said, "I'm not going to stay here. I'm putting in for a transfer. I'm not living in a shit ass tent."

Another of the guys was a southern boy; as yet he hadn't said anything but was known to always find something good in any situation.

"Yuall," he said, "we've been had, but it could be worse."

"Yah—how?"

"Well, for one thing it could be raining."

"Shit."

"And for another, we could have been split up at Schrusbury, but we're together; we're in a combat group, which is what we been bustin' our ass for, so let's quit bitchin' and report to the group commander. Or we could resign, which would mean turning in our wings, or we might appeal, or . . ."

"Okay, for Christ's sake, knock it off; let's go meet the guy who runs this dump." But the group commander was too busy to welcome us; that was handled by his executive officer. He assigned us to our squadrons—three of us to one and one to one of the other two squadrons. With three out of the four going to one squadron we figured that outfit was either the most aggressive, most unlucky, or made up of the worst pilots. None of these assumptions proved correct. They had had some tough missions and paid the price in losses.

A jeep took the three of us and our luggage to squadron headquarters—which was a tent—but the squadron commander was too busy to greet us; that was left to the operations officer. He assigned us to different flights but didn't assign us any particular quarters. He showed us where the pilots lived and told us to find a place for ourselves.

It seemed nobody cared about us or were in any way interested in us. We had to find our own way to the mess tent for lunch, and when we got there, couldn't eat because we didn't have a mess kit.

So much for the Hollywood version. Now we were in the real world; may as well face it, this is the way it is. What we didn't know was that shortly it was going to get worse when the group started its move to France. The big tents came down, and we moved into our individual pup tents. When they issued them to us in the States as part of our standard gear, I thought, why are they giving us these? We'll be living in a semi-castle. I should have known, but I'd seen all the Hollywood movies and couldn't believe anything else.

Another thing we'd been issued in the States was a tin hat, a regular army steel helmet. Although we thought it would make a good butt can, it turned out to be priceless. The buzz bombs were on four channels coming right over our field on the way to London. They carried a 1,000-pound warhead, flew about 400 feet above the ground, and cruised at 500 miles per hour.

The British had antiaircraft batteries at the coast and for a few miles inland. Then there was a free zone where the R.A.F. operated, flying Spitfires and Hurricane fighters. These planes had been stripped of armament and all excess weight and had beefed up engines; they were fast—about as fast as the buzz bombs. They would patrol at 2,500 feet, and when they spotted a buzz bomb, they'd dive to get speed, catch up to it from the rear, and shoot it down. The only trouble for us was that it still had its 1,000 pound warhead. We took plenty of hits from them but never a casualty; although, one blew up our mess tent, and another hit in the middle of our maintenance and repair area and knocked out five Thunderbolts.

One afternoon we were watching a Spitfire attack one. The pilot had so much speed from his dive that he was overrunning the buzz bomb, so he fired. The whole thing blew up—remaining fuel and the warhead—and he flew right through the debris; it was a giant ball of fire. He came out the other end and was on fire himself. He spotted our field, dropped his wheels, made a short turn, and landed. Our emergency crew put the fire out, and he was okay.

Actually there was only moderate damage to the plane. The R.A.F. flew in a mechanic with a new prop, and the plane was repaired and flown out the next day. But that gave us a first hand look at the Spitfire, and although it was a damn good fighter, I was glad that I was in a Thunderbolt. The Spits did ground support, but they must have taken heavy losses.

So there we were, finally in the Big Time. After 17 months of continual training we were ready to become air warriors, and we couldn't wait. But wait we did. A new replacement pilot, unless desperately needed immediately, was allowed to hang around awhile, get settled in, and watch a few missions come and go. During our waiting period we were checked out by the operations officer in a formation flight so he could evaluate our skill as pilots. I got some flights breaking in new engines. It was called Slow-Time. After an engine was replaced it had to be flown at reduced speed for a few hours, then at a higher speed for a few more, and gradually increased to full power. This was not the most glamorous assignment in the squadron, but it was a necessary one; therefore, it was given to the lowest ones on the totem pole, newly arrived, 2nd lieutenant replacement pilots.

I had one opportunity to add some spice to this tedium. I was flying about 5,000 feet just roaming around the area when I saw the flak batteries open up. It had to be a buzz bomb coming through. Finally I spotted it way below me and moving very fast. I couldn't power dive as that would overspeed the engine, so I chopped the throttle to idle and started down trying to time my dive and turn. I was already relishing the glory of shooting it down. Well that didn't happen, by the time I got down to 2,000 feet that thing was long gone. There was no Spitfire on his tail either, so that one probably got to London.

A week later I was finally put on the schedule. I was going to fly my first combat mission. I was so elated I forgot to be scared.

I suppose every pilot, until his dying day, will remember his first mission, which could have been his first and last combat mission. Actually, though, very few pilots were lost on their first one, although no effort was made to wait for a milk run for a new guy. He was there because he wanted to be, and he was ready to go.

We, the replacements that is, were trained as high-altitude, bomber escort, fighter pilots. Only after arriving in England were we given any low-altitude strafing training and never any dive-bombing training. This may have been for security reasons because the pending massive use of fighter-bombers, which had already been planned for the invasion and march across Europe, was a closely held secret. Fighter-bombers had been used in the North African campaign, but the concept of air-ground support, which was planned for the European campaign, was fighter aircraft working with infantry and armored troops on a regular basis at the front lines at near ground level, and that was new. Extensive training by the air corps in this technique could have given the German high command advance notice.

I thought at the time it was for this reason that we were committed to this extremely dangerous form of combat without any training. The only other reason would be that the training command was completely out of touch with the operational command, and the left hand didn't know what the right hand was doing. Research after the war proved that to be the case. In any event, hundreds of fighter-bomber pilots dropped their first bomb on a heavily defended enemy target while flying their first combat mission.

Initially the squadrons experienced heavy losses because they hadn't developed a technique to use evasive tactics and still get into the target. My first mission was a perfect example.

It was a combination bomber escort and dive-bomb group mission. We were to rendezvous with a group of B-26 bombers over the English Channel at 15,000 feet. The next phase was escort. We would stay with them until shortly before we reached the target. Hopefully, as far as we were concerned, they'd be attacked by enemy fighters, and we'd be able to jettison our external tanks and belly bomb and engage the famed Luftwaffe and shoot them down. Unfortunately the Luftwaffe didn't show up, so we were still prepared for the final phase, which was to leave the bombers 10 minutes before reaching the target and go on ahead to attack the antiaircraft guns. We were to obliterate these guns so the bombers could come in at about 8,000 feet and destroy a bridge across the Loire River.

This particular target had been bombed before by the B-26s (twin-engine medium bombers), but the flak was so heavy the bombardiers got nervous at 25,000 and missed it. This time, with the flak guns knocked out, they flew in at 8,000 feet and blew it to pieces. But back to my first bomb drop.

As bombers approach their target, the bombardier actually takes over control of the aircraft. He must get the plane lined up, correct for wind, and bring the plane to the precise point in the sky so that the bombs, when released, will fall directly onto the target. He cannot dodge flak during this bomb run. The only hope is that the flak will miss his plane. He must fly straight and level and continue on regardless of the flak; it's called asshole-pucker-time.

When the Thunderbolt groups, who were later to join the Ninth Air Force in Europe, began training in the States, they adopted the navy method of dive-bombing. They simply located the target, rolled over, and came straight at it. That was okay because nobody was shooting at them. Later when they arrived in Europe and were committed to combat, they used the same technique they had used in training. This was okay for awhile because many of the targets were not defended by antiaircraft guns. But after D-Day, when the war really got started, thousands of German troops were brought into the battle area along with an oversupply of antiaircraft guns, and from then on every target was heavily defended.

But the good old boys by now were steeped in their tradition of the straight in approach. They'd peel off from 25,000 feet and dive directly at the target. They were doing the same thing the bomber boys were doing except they were diving directly into the guns. This stupid tactic took its toll.

There was no bomb sight on the Thunderbolt; you simply pointed the nose of the plane directly at the target, and when you were a heartbeat away, you released the bomb and pulled out of the dive.

So my first bomb run was a textbook example from the navy training manual. I identified my target, which was an 88-millimeter antiaircraft gun, rolled over from 25,000 feet, and headed straight for him. It took him just a few seconds to nail me on the way in. Fortunately it was not a mortal wound, at least not then, and I continued on the bomb run, planting my 500-pound, general purpose, instantaneous fused bomb right in his lap, which immediately became fertilizer for the surrounding countryside along with the gun and the rest of the gun crew.

I did make it back to England, but just barely, crashing a mile or so beyond the deadly clutches of the English Channel. To get knocked out of the box your first time up doesn't do great things for your self-esteem, so I vowed I'd figure a less lethal way of getting into a target in the future. But old traditions die hard, and it took awhile.

Any suggestions by a replacement pilot, especially one involving combat tactics, were received by the old boys about as graciously as a bout of diarrhea. But there was enough space between planes during the dive-bomb run to allow for some individuality. We, the replacement pilots, talked it over and decided to try something different. We began to constantly change the angle of the dive, skid sideways, half-roll away from the target, and anything and everything to confuse the gunners on the ground. Only at the very last second did you straighten out the plane and head directly for the target.

Gradually, very gradually, this approach became the norm, and the old boys were telling us that this was the best way to get into a heavily defended target. We accepted their tutelage with a straight face, and sometimes laughingly wondered if they really did believe they had invented it. In any event it was a great improvement over the navy style and undoubtedly saved many pilots.

# chapter 6

# TRANSITION

Prior to D-Day there were 12 P-47 Thunderbolt fighter-bomber groups operating from bases in England; by the end of the war the number had grown to 15. A group in the air consisted of three squadrons of 12 planes each for a total of 36 planes. On occasion the group would add an extra flight to each squadron for a total of 48. That meant on a given day of maximum effort, the Ninth Air Force, prior to D-Day, could put 576 Thunderbolts on targets in France.

Their primary mission at that phase of the war was interdiction. That meant sealing off what was to become, after D-Day, the battleground. In order not to give the actual invasion location away, no special targeting emphasis was given to Cherbourg or Caen. The Allied stratagem was to make the Germans believe the invasion would occur in the Calais area, which was the closest point between England and France. To this end, many missions were flown to that area.

Mission targets were bridges, railroad marshaling yards, stores of supplies, and troop concentrations, wherever they existed. Every piece of equipment destroyed, every German killed, would be that much less our invasion forces would have to face. Railroad trains were particularly vulnerable to fighter-bomber attack. The steam locomotive was easy to spot with its telltale plume of white; it became the favorite target of the Fighter-Bomber Boys.

A typical attack would be made from the side on the locomotive. Bombs would be used if still available, but they were not necessary because the 50-caliber machine guns would easily penetrate the boiler causing an explosion and disabling the train. Bombs had the advantage of blowing the locomotive off the tracks causing many of the cars to derail and topple and also destroying some track, which made repairs and salvage operations more difficult for the Germans. Once the locomotive was destroyed, it was a turkey shoot. Each plane, in turn, would pick the next rail car in line and attack with all guns blazing. The pilot would then make a climbing turn to about 400 feet, circle around the train, and come in again. Everyone stayed in position following the plane ahead of him; traffic discipline was mandatory to avoid midair collisions or possibly shooting another plane in the squadron. The cars usually caught fire or exploded, but the attack would continue until the entire train was destroyed.

# CHAPTER 6: TRANSITION

However, one day there was a surprise. The squadron leader had exploded the locomotive, and the squadron was now in trail with each plane coming in on the next car in line when all at once we came under intense heavy fire. The radio came alive.

"Where the hell's that flak coming from."

"Bonebreak squadron, break off. Assemble angels 10 [10,000 feet] south of the train."

We all scattered, headed south, climbed to 10,000 feet, and rejoined formation. At this altitude we were well out of range of the 20-millimeter flak they were shooting.

"Bonebreak leader, this is Blue leader. One of those is a flat car loaded with 20s."

We had now returned to the train, were circling above it, and trying to figure out what happened.

"Bonebreak leader, this is Yellow leader. There were no flat cars when we started the attack."

Someone cut in, "Then where the hell did it come from?"

"This is Bonebreak leader. Who has bombs left? Acknowledge."

"Bonebreak leader, this is Blue three; three and four have bombs."

"Bonebreak squadron stand by."

This was something new, and the squadron leader was trying to figure out how to handle it. Then he came on the radio.

"Bonebreak squadron, this is Bonebreak leader. Red and Blue flight will attack line abreast. Blue three and four, bomb the guns. Yellow flight attack the guns after Blue three and four have bombed. Has everybody got that? Flight leaders acknowledge."

"Yellow leader—roger."

"Bonebreak leader from Blue leader. Are you going in on the locomotive side?"

"Roger, Blue leader."

"Blue three, you understand your position, I'll move to the left."

"Blue three, roger."

"Arm your bombs."

The attack came off as planned. The flak guns were knocked out, and the rest of the train strafed.

The Germans were a formidable adversary, and when their railroad trains became prime targets, they devised a defense. Their ingenious idea was a special car equipped with collapsible sides and top and armed with several of the dreaded quadmount 20-millimeter flak guns. They knew that after we blew up the engine, disabling the train, we'd get into a tight strafing pattern and slow our speed to under 300 miles per hour; we were then vulnerable. Suddenly the top and sides would come down, and instantly there were 20-millimeter flak guns firing.

The incident of the flak car was spread to all fighter-bomber groups, and from then on every train was considered by every squadron to have a flak car. Attack strategy was immediately changed. The squadrons spread out, putting more distance between planes, and increased speed strafing, but mainly they saved a few bombs. When the flak car exposed itself, the squadron would pull away, and the plane or flight with bombs would move out of range, gain altitude, usually to at least 10,000 feet, and then dive-bomb the flak car. One direct hit, or even a near miss, was all that was necessary, and the squadron would return to the kill and strafe.

So, as is usual in war, the addition of the flak car did not change the outcome of the battle; it simply made it more vicious and increased the death count. But I'll say for sure that those gunners on the flak cars were gutsy bastards. They fought courageously even though they were nearly certain of being killed or severely wounded.

Bridges were priority targets. Blow the bridge and transportation came to a standstill. Every bridge spanning the Loire River was destroyed. This actually split the German army, denying them rapid movement of troops from north to south after the land fighting started. I'll cover this in detail in chapter 8, "General's Decision."

Bridges were difficult to destroy for two reasons: the span itself was narrow—only two lanes—and the abutments were heavy concrete. The navy dive-bombing technique just didn't work, so new tactics were devised. It was damn disappointing to haul bombs all the way from England, fly over enemy territory, wade through some flak, and then miss the bridge. There had to be a better way, and there was: we called it Drive Bombing; it was definitely different. To begin with, the bombs had 8- to 11-second delayed fuses. The dive was started at least a mile away from the bridge to level out just over the river about 500 yards from the bridge. At that point your speed was about 450 miles per hour, and you were flying below the level of the bridge, just above the water, and straight for the abutment. At the last split second you pulled up and released the bomb, clearing the bridge by a hair's breadth. The bomb continued on, crashing into the abutment at 400 miles per hour and burrowed into the structure. When it exploded, because it was practically encapsulated, the entire abutment disintegrated, resulting in the collapse of the span. This method proved highly successful and a real test of the pilot's timing and flying skill. On the down side, your life depended on the accuracy of the delayed fuse mechanism; if it malfunctioned and exploded on contact—you went up with the bomb. But to my knowledge no such accident ever happened.

Most groups continued these interdiction missions as long as they were flying from England, but the mission requirement was rapidly changing as our ground troops got a foothold in France. Now it was time for Eisenhower to use his Thunderbolts to support those ground troops, and he did. The tough, deadly work was about to begin.

# chapter 7

# FUN TIME

In spite of the fact that the pilots faced death constantly, they had a lot of fun times, and there was some irresponsibility in their attitude to everything but flying. If there was any devilment they could get into and it looked like fun, they did it.

Our first airfield in France was built in an apple orchard, and the owner of the orchard also ran some cattle there. We had run out of whiskey, and even our personal, private stock was fast being depleted. Someone stole a supply of alcohol and said he knew how to make it drinkable if we could find some fruit juice. Someone else produced the fruit juice.

This called for a party; we scrounged wood for a campfire, and someone—but no one ever admitted to it—shot one of the farmer's cows. I think it was a guy from Texas because he knew how to cut it up in all the right pieces, and we had a barbecue.

We all sat around drinking that rotgut and eating French cow until everyone passed out. The repercussions the next day were major. The squadron commander demanded to know who shot the cow, but no one would tell him, and the flight surgeon had a fit because we were all sick from that straight alcohol. Fortunately the squadron was on a stand-down for repairs, so there was no mission that day.

The farmer, owner of the cow, pushed his complaint to the group commander, and in order to avoid a big flap we offered to buy the cow, but somehow it blew over in time, and no one ever shot another cow or drank straight alcohol again—but it was a blast.

There was a guy in a nearby group who was really a Don Juan; if women were anywhere around, he could find them. As soon as he got to France, he began to prowl and discovered an evacuation hospital not far from us.

On his own he set up a big party and invited some of our guys. When everything was set, he informed us that he'd lined up about 30 nurses, and the party was on. He was a real promoter, even arranging for the trucks to pick them up and take them home again. There was just one problem for us: with only 30 nurses, there wouldn't be enough to go around, so the new boys were excluded. But even if we hadn't been, most of us would not have gone. It doesn't pay for a 2nd lieutenant wing man to cut in on his squadron commander or flight leader while he is dancing with a nurse—even if she's only a 2nd lieutenant.

The party was a huge success. There was a record player, plenty of booze and food, and the nurses were impressed. We didn't find out until the next morning that there had been a tragedy. While the nurses were being returned to their hospital, one of the trucks turned over, and several of them were injured, some seriously. They had plans for one of these parties once a week, but the accident put the lid on that, and the nurses were placed "off limits." Both the nurses and the pilots considered this overkill, but the responsible commanders were anxious to cover their tails. So what could have been great for the morale of ourselves and the nurses was stifled by the brass. Of course, it didn't matter a hell of a lot to us because we couldn't go anyway, but we were sorry the nurses were injured.

Our field in England was only a couple of hours by train from London, and we got three-day leaves fairly often, but once we arrived in France it was a different story. Where could you go in three days—nowhere—because all of the towns that had been liberated were blown to hell. So the policy was changed to suit the circumstances; we got leave less frequently but for a longer period, usually one week plus travel time to and from London.

Finally my turn came, and my buddy Jim was also going. We intended to spend that time in the pursuit of pretty women, drinking plenty of good booze, eating excellent meals in fine restaurants, and staying at deluxe hotels. That would be a welcome change from living in a tent, eating out of a mess kit, and wading around in the mud.

There were five of us on the leave schedule, one of which was a flight leader. It would be his unpleasant responsibility to see that we all got back on time.

Before leaving the squadron, the flight surgeon called us to his tent and gave us three things: a fifth of whiskey each, a box containing a gross of rubbers (now called condoms), and a lecture about V.D. He told us he'd not be pleased if any of us came back with a dose of clap (gonorrhea). We listened to his lecture and took our bottle of booze. I was put in charge of the rubbers; we'd divvy them up later.

We went by open truck to an air transport field near Cherbourg. The place was loaded with C-47s, and the operations shack was crowded with military personnel awaiting transport to England. We figured, because we were practically conquering heroes, that we'd get right on a flight for England. The dispatcher, however, had different ideas. Being harassed from all sides, he was not too interested in our travel plans or quasi-hero status. He checked our orders, added our names to his list, and told us to wait. Two hours went by, and we were still waiting. Each hour here was an hour less in London and an hour of precious leave time used up. Our highest rank was our flight leader, but he was only a 1st lieutenant. There were majors and colonels waiting ahead of us.

Four hours went by, and we were still waiting.

"Okay, enough of this bullshit. We've got to make a plan to get outta here. Our first day's damn near shot. We'll never get to London at this rate. Who's got an idea?"

Things were silent for awhile. Finally one of the guys spoke up.

"There's some C-47s sitting over there by themselves; maybe we could swipe one."

"Damn good idea," said somebody else.

"Wait a minute," said the flight leader who was technically in charge of our little group. "Who the hell's going to fly it? Who's checked out in a C-47?"

"Come on," somebody said. "We can fly the son of a bitch if we can just get it started."

"Well who the hell knows how to start it?"

There was a prolonged silence. Obviously—although a great idea—it wouldn't work. More silence.

"Look you guys, let's find out who's in charge of this flight line and go to him. That God damn sergeant doesn't care about us, but maybe the officer in charge might."

Everyone seemed to agree with this idea, but I was skeptical.

"Listen, if we're going to talk to anyone, it should be the base commander. I'm sure he'd give us some consideration. God damn it, we ought to have some kind of priority."

As soon as I opened my mouth, I knew I'd been elected. "Okay, I'll go," I said, and started for base headquarters.

On the way I saw a familiar face with major's leaves on his uniform. This familiar face belonged to a famous race car driver of pre-war days, Ronnie Householder. As a teenager I had hung around his shop after school and on weekends until I finally got on his pit crew. So here we met in the middle of a war.

"Ronnie, what the hell are you doing here?"

Being called by his first name was startling to the major, and he looked all around trying to identify the offender. I kept walking straight for him, and he finally recognized me.

"Tom, you're a fly boy. What are you doing here?"

"I asked first," I said.

"I'm just playing around with old iron. But what about you? What are you flying?"

"Thunderbolts, and I'm on my way to find the base commander. There's five of us on leave, and we can't get out of this place. We're trying to get to London. We've been waiting for four hours and can't get a plane out."

"You don't need the base commander. Come on. I'm on my way to operations. I'll fix you up."

When we got there, he picked up a couple of clipboards and ran his fingers down the names. Each clipboard held the list of passengers for the flights out. It took him a couple of minutes to rearrange things; he simply crossed out five names, wrote ours in, and added the cross-outs to a later list. He then handed the clipboards back to the dispatcher, and that was that. We were on the next flight out.

Householder had the important job of examining battle damaged tanks and armored vehicles that were pulled back from the front to the Cherbourg area. He decided which ones could be repaired; the others were scrapped for parts. This meant expediting the movement of mechanics, technicians, and parts between England and that base. That fortunately allowed him to arrange transportation schedules. I thanked him profusely and told him I'd see him back at his race car shop after the war. He looked at my wings and my Ninth Air Force shoulder patch and said, "Good luck. I hope you make it."

The guys were amazed that I was able to work such magic. I explained that it was purely a lucky circumstance, but that didn't diminish their appreciation. According to them, I was the guy who knew big wheels. I did keep that meeting. After the war I went back to Householder's race car shop to say hello. I wanted him to know I'd made it.

When we arrived at Waterloo Station in London, Jim and I hung together. I don't recall how the other guys teamed up. Anyway, I had the rubbers, so we all stood around the waiting room in the station while I dutifully opened the box and gave each guy 28. If anyone noticed our rather bizarre activity, like good Britons, they looked the other way.

Jim and I got quarters at a hotel in Piccadilly and immediately went on the prowl. My initiation into the fleshpots of London had made me wary; we weren't interested in picking up hookers. But this time we were armed with better intelligence and had clearly defined targets.

The British had a military organization called the A.T.S. It was an all female affair, and the letters stood for the Allied Territorial Service, but we called it the American Tail Service. As we searched around the side streets near Piccadilly, we came upon two little dolls in A.T.S. uniforms sauntering down the avenue.

"Which one do you want?" Jim asked.

"I'll take the one on the left."

"Good."

We came up behind them so we'd end up on the side of the one we chose.

"Hi, girls. Where you headed?"

"Nowhere, Yank. Just out for a walk."

"We're here on a week's leave. Can you show us around?" They stopped and looked at us, then at each other, apparently satisfied with the selection, and Jim's girl said, "What do you want to do?" It was such a leading question my girl laughed. So we headed for the nearest pub. The place was mobbed, but we finally found a table, and just as we sat down, an M.P. tapped Jim on the shoulder.

"Sir, officers are not allowed to associate with enlisted personnel."

"We're really not associating, just sitting at the same table. Isn't that okay?"

"I'm sorry, sir. Either the girls have to leave the table, or you'll all have to leave this place."

I could see we couldn't win, so I said, "Let's go. We'll go to our hotel. We've got plenty of booze there."

So we did, but as we walked across the lobby and toward the elevator, the night clerk came running from behind the counter and blocked our path.

"This is an officers' billet," he began. "No enlisted personnel allowed." Then he took on the air of the prissy headmaster, "And further, women are not allowed in the gentlemen's quarters—no exceptions."

True, this was a military hotel. When on official leave, you stayed free. While Jim and I were arguing with this little pip-squeak, the girls were quietly talking.

"Come on," one of them said. "Let's go outside."

When we got to the sidewalk, the girls suggested we go to their quarters, and they would change into civilian clothes. But they had other plans, too.

When we got to their place, they had us wait outside, kind of semi-hiding in some trees. In a few minutes they came out and motioned to us to follow them. They went to the side of the building and looked up. Someone on the second floor opened a window and tossed out a couple of overnight bags. They already knew we'd be in London for a week, and they told us they were going A.W.O.L. (absent without leave) until we left.

They knew the city and took us to an area where we could rent a flat for the week. There they changed into civilian clothes; we got a cab, went back to our hotel, got our clothes, booze, and 56 rubbers, and returned to our rented flat. The girls explained they'd been up since 5:00 A.M. and had to get some sleep, so we called it a night. For the next week we lived it up. Jim and I each had two months' pay, and we intended to spend it. The girls loved it. Their life in the A.T.S. was very drab and dull. We spent most of the day in the sack, and at night we hit the hotels for dinner and the clubs for drinking and dancing.

English food is not the greatest at best, and during the war it was downright awful, but we did manage a few black market steaks, and we also learned that English chips were really french fries.

Unfortunately, it finally came time to say good-bye. The girls told us they'd be put on detention when they returned, but their short fling with us had been worth it. When we left London, we were out of booze, nearly out of money, but still had 56 rubbers. Somehow the thought of those dolls having a dose just didn't make sense; besides that, penicillin had just been invented, and clap was easier to cure than the common cold. Fortunately we returned to the squadron with neither.

Our leave was typical. Doing the kind of flying the Fighter-Bomber Boys were doing, there was an acceptance that death could come at any time. When they were lucky enough to go on leave, it was all out for fun and that not only included, but centered around, sex. The majority of pilots were 21 to 23 years old with a full 90 percent under 25. With raging hormones, an uncertain tomorrow, plenty of money, and available women, the quadrangle was complete with sex in the center.

If a pilot returned from leave with stories of sightseeing and evenings spent at the theater or in an English pub, the flight surgeon would have sent him for a psychiatric examination. The degree of success of a leave was directly proportional to the number of times the pilot got laid. To further this purpose, girls' names, such as the ones we spent our time with while on leave, were often given to other members of the squadron or friends in other squadrons.

The girls who were our partners in this liaison were certainly not trollops. After all, they were young and healthy. They had survived the vicious bombing of London and were now enduring the lethal buzz bombs and V2 attacks. Their lives were very much in harm's way. Duty hours were long, and life was dull. The chance to spend time with the glamorous fly boys was too much to turn down. They were proper English girls doing their duty for God and country and could see nothing wrong with having as much fun as possible while doing it.

You might consider it as a grassroots way of promoting Anglo-American wartime cooperation—we did.

# chapter 8
# THE GENERAL'S DECISION

The Eighth Air Force, as I have previously described, was the strategic air force. Its strategy was its own, being formulated in Washington, and was not under General Eisenhower's direct authority. The Ninth Air Force was the tactical air force and, in reality, an extension of the ground forces. By that I mean the fighter-bomber was a weapons system used in support of the ground troops, and although it was under the command of Ninth Air Force generals, targets were selected based on requests from army commanders.

General George S. "Blood and Guts" Patton, commanded the Third Army and was, in my humble opinion, the best combat general we had in Europe. The XIX Tactical Air Command flew in support of the Third Army. General Patton understood the capabilities of the fighter-bomber and knew how best to use them.

The following is a quote from his book *War As I Knew It.* "I asked General Weyland, commanding general of the XIX Tactical Air Command, to send some fighter-bombers to stop it [a column of German tanks]. The bombers [P-47s] were unable to find the column, because it actually was the 4th Armored Division moving in from the northeast. However, the planes did do some very effective work knocking out enemy resistance ahead of the 4th Armored Division and this was the precursor of many other such jobs. It was love at first sight between the XIX Tactical Air Command and the Third Army" **(96).**

Please bear in mind that General Patton was extremely reluctant to give any praise or credit to any military organization other than his very own Third Army. His admission that the P-47s effectively knocked out enemy resistance ahead of his forces was indeed a magnificent compliment.

As the battle progressed across central France, Patton kept his tanks and troops constantly on the attack, driving the Germans farther and farther back toward Germany. His right flank was the Loire River and was completely exposed to German forces who were south of that river and occupied that territory. At any time they could have come across the river and cut his lines, isolating his forward troops and setting up a classical pincer entrapment. With the forward elements cut off they could be easily slaughtered.

If you look at the battle maps of the European War, you will note that no American or Allied troops were ever positioned or fought south of the Loire, with the exception of a small force of Free French Fighters. Was Patton so foolhardy as to take such a calculated risk? No. He had one of the greatest weapons systems available at his disposal. He would use the P-47 fighter-bomber against any German forces daring to enter that territory.

It was in late August, we had been flying constantly and our planes had sustained heavy battle damage, so we had an extra day off so our ground crews could finish repairs. Interrupting our sack time the operation clerk came running into our tent area yelling for all pilots to report to the ready room; something must be up. The operation officer was weighting and had already posted the schedule of the pilots that would fly the mission. The French underground reported a very large formation of German troops had been spotted south of the Loire River. We were to find them, if they were really there, and destroy them; under the circumstances our day off had just been canceled. Even though some of our planes were still under repair there were enough ready to put the full squadron in the air.

We arrived in the battle area late in the afternoon and could not believe what we saw. There was a column of Germans as far as the eye could see. A division of German troops, with their supporting tanks, armored vehicles, and horse-drawn artillery; we began immediately to attack and to systematically cut them to ribbons. This was a real blood-

42

and-guts mission. The Germans were in retreat, and we caught them in open farm country. Their columns of tanks, armored vehicles, and personnel carriers were stretched for miles down the main road heading east. The fields next to the roads were crawling with infantry.

The first thing I noticed, because I hadn't seen them before, was the horse-drawn caissons. It was like something out of World War I.

With nowhere to hide, they had to fight, and fight they did. The Tiger tank with its deadly 88 was one hell of a weapon, but the gunners couldn't seem to handle it too well against us. This is understandable when you consider the tank was moving taking evasive action, and we were moving, skidding and slipping, twisting and turning, until the very last second before shooting. It was suicide to fly a straight direct line attack into a tank; the tank gunner could get a direct bead on you, and the 88 would blow you out of the sky.

In a big battle like this the squadron loses some sense of control. The antiaircraft fire was fierce, with explosions and fire all over the place, and we were spread out for a couple of miles over their column, 12 planes diving, shooting, climbing, and diving again for another attack; the noise was deafening, This was low-level fighting at its deadliest After pulling off the target we never climbed over 400 feet before making a tight turn and attacking again. It boiled down to getting into that column any way you could by dodging the flak that was coming your way. Then, when you were in perfect range, you slammed the controls to neutral to settle the airplane down and fired at what vehicle was in front of you. A 5-second burst was more than enough to totally destroy that target. Horses ran amok, and we shot them too. They were the unfortunate victims, but they carried ammunition and guns, and our job was to not let any of the troops, equipment, or supplies get away. We stayed until we expended all of our ammunition and then headed for home.

There was still one hell of a lot of German soldiers left so the following morning the entire group joined the battle. While our squadron carried on the slaughter in one section of the column, our other squadrons were doing the same thing a few miles up the road. When we withdrew and returned to base, the planes were quickly refueled, rearmed, we had some food, chain smoked, climbed back into the cockpit, returned to the battle area and continue the carnage.

There were burning vehicles stretched for miles, and bodies carpeted the roadway. By the third day the stench from the battlefield was so bad, you could smell it in the cockpit. Bloated horse carcasses with stiff legs pointed skyward were unpleasant to see; the horses were not our enemy

The battle lasted for three days. In one day alone our group destroyed over 600 vehicles; these included tanks, armored personnel carriers, half-tracks, and trucks of every description. The cost in human life to the German army was staggering. This was a battle scene that would live in memory, but barely a word of it has ever been published.

As with all battles, eventually it ended and so did this historic event. At briefing on the fourth morning we were told that the Germans were surrendering and to circle over the town of Tours at 700 feet but not to attack unless ordered to by our ground controller. With a squadron of fighter bombers overhead there was no fight left in them and we were soon released and returned to our regular hunting grounds looking for fresh targets

The official surrender ceremony took place at Issoudun, France on September 10 1944 General Botho Elster Commander Group Marschgruppe Sud Southern Group had offered an unconditional surrender. His army had numbered 20,000 at the beginning of the battle. In three days we had cut that number in half with approximately 7,000 killed and 3,000 severely wounded. The surrender was accepted by Major General Robert C. Macon Commanding General of the 83rd Infantry division 9th US Army. The surrender took place at Issoudun, France, on the 10 September,1944. General Patton's Third Army was not involved in the actual surrender ceremony. By this time he was many miles to the east on his way to Germany, but he states in his book, *War As I knew It*, "they surrendered to the Third Army and the XIX Tactical Air Command".

Patton makes note of this unusual event in his book *War As I Knew It*, saying that the German General wanted it specifically understood t h a t  he was surrendering to the P-47 Thunderbolts. No ground forces had fired so much as a shot at the German troops, and as near as anyone knew at the time, it was the only time in the history of warfare that a large, completely equipped army had been defeated by air attack alone to the point that surrender was the only course left open co them.

Years later I met a lieutenant colonel who was one of the team General Patton sent to observe that surrender. He was utterly amazed that this had been accomplished without the use of any ground troops. He freely admitted that from then on he had a healthy respect and deep admiration for the P-47 fighter-bombers and the pilots who flew them.

This great victory was due to General Patton's ability to select the right weapons and the right tactics to be used in a given situation against the enemy. It was also due to the skill and courage of the pilots who flew the missions and the unbeatable characteristics of the P-47 as a weapons system for air-to-ground fighting.

Our group was awarded the Presidential Unit Citation, and in addition the general showed his appreciation by sending a case of Cointreau to every pilot and a bottle of Cointreau to every enlisted man in the squadron.

There are several things significant in the foregoing. It tells something of Patton's understanding, first, of fighting men; they liked to drink; second, of his deep ingrained belief that there was a distinct separation between officers and enlisted men and an even greater separation between those who actually engaged in com- bat and those who were in a support role; and finally, that killing Germans lots, of Germans, was an honorable endeavor.

But that's not the end of the story. About a week after the surrender we were invited by the mayor, the people of Tours, and the Free French Freedom Fighters as their guests for a victory celebration. We were given the day off and left early in trucks. The food situation for the French was tough, so we brought lots of canned foods and bread. It was a long uncomfortable ride, but no one objected because we went right through the battle area where we had flown missions in support of Patton's troops a few weeks earlier. It gave us a first-hand view of what devastation results when air and ground work together. We also got to see and examine the dreaded quadmount 20-millimeter and 88 millimeter antiaircraft guns. The empty shell casing from the 88 stood nearly three feet tall, and the projectile was more than a foot long and bigger than your fist. Wow! Is this what they shoot at us? No wonder a direct hit can disintegrate a Thunderbolt and leave nothing but small pieces of junk fluttering to the ground. We had a healthy respect for the 88 anyway, and this first-hand look reinforced it. We did, however, see a further use for the spent casings. We brought a dozen back with us and used them for stand-up ashtrays in the pilots' ready-room.

When we arrived in Tours, we were taken first to the headquarters of the Free French Freedom Fighters. They were called the Machy. I believe that was a nickname derived from the French word meaning to oppose. As we approached the place, I was awestruck. I was about to enter into a French Foreign Legion movie set. Here it was, a fortress with high embattlement walls and a gate tower. We entered through the gate and saw a large earth-packed quadrangle with low barracks built next to the walls on three sides. The top of the barracks served as battle positions for the embattlements.

We were taken up into the gate tower, through narrow passages and small rooms, and finally into the presence of a dazzlingly beautiful woman. She introduced herself as the commandant's secretary and led us into his office. There were about 20 of us who squeezed into his office. He greeted us in a very reserved manner, she acted as interpreter. He was in full dress uniform with medals displayed, wearing that ridiculous French bellboy's hat. We were in dirty flight suits and G.I. shoes, which were rather seedy looking compared to his highly polished leather boots. He told us, through her, that the men were in barracks and eagerly looking forward to meeting us, and we should feel free to mingle with them. His statement was in the form of a mild dismissal, and she led us out. He was a pompous son of a bitch, but he sure knew gorgeous female flesh; later we would find out more about that.

We then went to the barracks and met the shabbiest bunch of men I ever saw who were supposed to be soldiers. Most were in civilian clothes, and they showed us a variety of French, German, and English weapons that they used. They told us they watched our battle, but admitted they did damn little fighting themselves. They would cross the river at night, go on a short patrol, and if they ran into Germans, they'd shoot and then withdraw back to their barracks where they'd drink wine and bed their girlfriends. The war was a game to them: fight a little, enjoy their women a lot, and drink plenty. We asked about the commandant's secretary, and they all laughed and told us she was his private stock, and they were never allowed to go into the gate tower. These guys were not in the army; they were civilians who fought when they felt like it and goofed off when they felt like it. They did a commendable job in many parts of France, but here, as they laughingly explained to us, they saw no need to get involved because we were doing such a good job of killing Germans.

At 3:00 in the afternoon we went to the main hotel in town where a dinner had been arranged in the main ballroom, and it was then that we met the townspeople and city officials. There were toasts and speeches, most of which were given through an interpreter, and food. The people were very nice to us, and we all enjoyed the celebration. After the meal a guy who spoke a little English came up to me and handed me a knife. He said he was one of the Machy and had taken the knife from a German soldier that he had killed. He wanted to trade it for my 45 pistol. Of course I couldn't do that, but I wanted the knife, so we dickered for awhile. He really wanted my pistol, but I told him I couldn't give away army property without getting in trouble. I finally offered him my wings, and I could see he was almost ready to accept, so to make sure, I threw in a pack of Lucky Strike cigarettes, and the deal was made. Years later I found out that the knife was a prized British Commando knife. So what was the history of that trophy? Did a German kill a British Commando and take the knife as a prize and then lose his life and the knife to a French Machy, who in turn traded it to me for a pair of silver wings and a pack of cigarettes? Who knows? But I still have the knife, and it's one of my most precious souvenirs.

Well, the celebration finally concluded. We all had too much wine, which made the trip back to our base miserable, plus a full-blown headache and a queasy stomach. But somehow we survived and had a very interesting and unusual experience, and it sure opened our eyes to the Frenchman's attitude toward life and war. He seemed to say, "Why be in a hurry? The fighting will wait. Let's eat, drink, and be merry, and let tomorrow take care of itself." Of course, you will recall that the Germans defeated them in very short order and without much trouble.

After seeing how tenaciously the British had resisted Hitler's onslaught, the bravery of the English people during the bombing of Britain, and the unquestioned devotion to duty of the R.A.F. pilots in the Battle of Britain, I found it difficult to have much respect for France. There were, however, countless numbers of French people who, at great risk to themselves, saved a number of American and English flyers. They hid them from the Germans, fed and clothed them, and passed them through their resistance organization until they were safely returned to England or crossed the Alps into neutral territory. These were the French patriots, and they had our undying respect and gratitude.

# chapter 9
# GOOD-BYE MY FRIEND

I met my friend when we first arrived at the Army Air Corps Basic Training Center. From there we went to a university for Aviation Student Training and then on to become Aviation Cadets. We stayed together throughout our pilot training, went overseas together, and ended up in the same combat squadron as fresh, new replacement pilots.

We were both convinced that no German son of a bitch could shoot us down; we were invincible. On my first mission I was shot down. This presented somewhat of a problem to us on our theory of invincibility. But because I survived, we altered our thinking slightly and agreed that they could, with a lucky shot, shoot us down but never kill us; we were still invincible.

Neither of us had any fear of combat flying. We were that sure of ourselves. By the end of our first month we had each flown about six or seven missions and saw no reason to change our minds. Not only were we invincible, we were immortal, and we would be the conquering heroes.

You must understand things as they were then—not as they are now. We were at war. If we lost the war, we would live under the heel of the Nazis and the Japs. No more cars, no more football games, no more Saturday night dances, no more Glen Miller, Tommy Dorsey, or Benny Goodman. Maybe our parents would be killed because they were too old to be of benefit to our new rulers. The stakes were high, and we knew it. Flying was voluntary; no one made you fly. You flew because you wanted to. You became a pilot because you felt you could best serve in that capacity. Your superior eyesight, learning ability, coordination, and guts belonged in a fighter cockpit. These characteristics were yours, but you owed them to your country. I never met a combat pilot who wouldn't willingly sacrifice his life for America—in those days, that is.

These concepts may be out of fashion now. Over the past several administrations our leaders have made a mockery out of honor, love of country, and personal integrity. Their hypocrisy must burn the souls of those gallant men of World War II. But this book is not about now. It is about then, and the values are the values of those days.

47

It was a narrow road bordered on both sides by high trees. A German armored column was retreating, and they must have thought the trees would give them concealment. One of the pilots spotted them, and the squadron leader ordered an attack. The first couple of vehicles in the lead were bombed, which prevented the others from continuing. The trees were so close together they couldn't maneuver and escape into the fields on either side. It was a classical trap. They were caught, and they knew it.

The attack was from the side, starting with the end vehicle and working up to the head of the column. As each plane dove, it took the next vehicle in line. Before a minute was up, there were tanks and half tracks on fire, and the ground was strewn with dead Germans. But it was anything but a one-way battle. They were fighting for their lives.

As my friend bored into a half-track armored vehicle with machine guns blazing, he was hit with antiaircraft fire, his plane went out of control, rolled over, and went into the ground upside down. His body was thrown from the plane a split second before it exploded.

In the military accounting—that means what we destroyed against what we lost—the mission was an overwhelming success. The squadron destroyed four Tiger tanks, a half dozen armored vehicles along with their crews, and most of a company of infantry that was with them—probably some 300 Germans; we lost one plane and one pilot.

Fortunately, I was not on that mission. I don't know how I would have reacted if I'd seen him go in, explode, and burn. I did learn a valuable lesson though: no one is invincible in combat. You use your best skills, bring every ounce of survival instincts to bear, but sometimes that's not enough. From then on combat flying got tougher for me. Each mission required more courage. It was a gradual thing, but it was relentless.

That night in the dark before I finally fell off to sleep, I told my friend goodbye, and I asked him to forgive me because I would not think of him again until after my combat flying days were over. I would have to forget his face, his infectious smile, his wonderful companionship, and the comfort and encouragement we had given each other during the tough training days of cadet school. We'd never sit and talk about our families again, get drunk together, go on the prowl for women. I'd never hear that dumb southern drawl that I used to kid him about but was so much a part of him. He was always able to find something good no matter how shitty the situation was. Such a waste, such a tragedy to snuff out a life so vibrant.

The cost of war is sometimes impossible to bear. If God is really on our side, how come he allows these things to happen? I'll miss you terribly, but I must forget you for now. I'm on the morning mission, and I can't afford a single instant of distraction; you know that. I've got to be 100 percent; no grieving, no day dreaming, nothing to interfere with the mission objective. And if you get this message, I know you'll understand.

The loss of such a close friend was physically and emotionally devastating, but it happened; the war went on, and you were still part of it. Grieving was not a good thing; grieving was a downer, and to be successful and survive, you had to be constantly upbeat, optimistic, and self-confident. Nearly everyone started out with a close buddy, but many of those relationships were cut short when one or the other was killed. We not only had to live through a war physically but emotionally as well.

New relationships were formed; you could not remain a loner. You made new buddies, and one would become your new best buddy. But I never again allowed myself to become so dependent on his company or emotional help. I built a wall. I hardened my shell. It was the only way you could survive.

I have talked to many Thunderbolt pilots over the years since the war, and everyone told me they experienced this emotional torment at least once during their combat flying. I thought I was unique. I wasn't. Amazingly enough, we all adopted the same defense; we just built a wall and didn't allow anyone to penetrate it. Oh, we still had buddies, but never again was there that deep emotional attachment that existed with the first one.

Some idiot somewhere in our higher command decided that we should hold memorial services for our pilots who had been killed in action. The first was to be held in August. By that time most of the fighter-bomber groups had been flying combat missions for about three months and had had many of their pilots killed. When this ceremony was announced, most of us thought it was a bad joke. But an order was actually given—All Personnel To Attend. That was the only order in my entire military career that I disobeyed, and I was joined by every pilot in our squadron. The subject was never brought up again.

# chapter 10

# SONG AND DANCE

It was the morning of our move; practically all equipment and personnel had gone except the 12 of us who were going to fly the last mission from this field. The mess tent was still up, but we were living in our individual pup tents—not exactly the greatest accommodations.

I kept my mess kit hanging from a pole in front of my tent, and when I wanted it for breakfast that morning, it was gone. I figured some jerk was trying to be funny, so I headed for the mess tent to find out. When I entered, I noticed a lot of extra people but didn't pay much attention and yelled, "Okay, who's the son of a bitch who took my mess kit?" Somebody yelled in return, "Watch your language. There are ladies present." And sure enough there were, but all these extra people were in army field uniforms, so they didn't stand out. I just hadn't noticed. Some guy got up from a table and came toward me and said, "It was me, but they said it would be okay." I looked at him in amazement and said, "You're Bing Crosby." He laughed and said he and his group had been kidnapped by my squadron the night before in Cherbourg. The squadron commander, along with the senior officers, had gone into Cherbourg, run into Crosby and his troop, and talked them into visiting us. Fred Astaire was with them. He had become separated from his U.S.O. tour group so came along with Crosby. After breakfast we all went over to our headquarters.

As I've mentioned before, our airfield had been built in the middle of an apple orchard and farm. Our headquarters building had been the land owner's home; he was permitted to live in the first two floors only; we used the rest. It was a dirty, white, five-story building set in a courtyard with several farm buildings in the same compound. Miraculously, it had escaped damage during the invasion.

Each floor was connected by an inside spiral stairwell, and at each floor there was also a foyer about eight feet by eight feet. On one side of this landing a door provided access to the rooms, and on the opposite side an open balcony overlooked the courtyard.

Combat operations was on the third floor; that was the hub of activity. The fourth floor was squadron administration, and the fifth floor, which looked like an afterthought perched on top of the building, was an oversized lookout tower; that was the pilots' ready-room. It was about 20 feet by 20 feet.

# CHAPTER 10: SONG AND DANCE

I was checking with combat operations to see if there had been any change in the mission status when my buddy Jim, who had just come from breakfast, arrived for the same purpose. Things were still the same: briefing at 1300 hours, take-off at 1400 hours. We went over to the balcony and watched the chickens scratching for food in the courtyard.

Soon we heard someone coming down the stairs, singing softly to himself. Because it was a circular stairway, you couldn't actually see anyone until they got near the landing in the foyer.

Anyway, this guy comes down the stairs, singing, arrives at our landing, says, "Hi, fellas," and keeps on going down the stairs. Jim turned to me with an astonished expression and said, "That guy looks just like Bing Crosby, sounds like him too. That was Bing Crosby." I realized that because of his late breakfast, he definitely wasn't aware of our visitors.

"Come on. For Christ's sake, get a grip on yourself. That guy's just another G.I. What the hell would Bing Crosby be doing here?"

"I swear he looked like Bing Crosby. Didn't you think?"

"No," I replied.

Soon we heard a steady tap, tap, tap, as someone else was descending the stairs, but he was two floors above us, so it took a while before he was at our level. He never broke his stride, just that steady tap, tap, tap as he rounded the corner, waved a mock salute, and said, "Hi, I'm getting my morning exercise." We watched him disappear down the stairs.

Jim looked at me with an expression of utter disbelief and positive recognition.

"That's Fred Astaire. I know that's Fred Astaire. Did you see him dance across that floor?"

I laughed and said, "First it's Bing Crosby; now it's Fred Astaire. Jim, I think you're getting flak happy—too many missions without a leave—better see the flight surgeon."

He had such a pained look I couldn't keep a straight face any longer, and I didn't want him to think he was going nuts. I laughed and said, "Okay, okay—it was Bing Crosby and Fred Astaire; they're here. The squadron commander and some of the other guys found them in Cherbourg last night and brought them here." He looked slightly relieved and slightly pleased.

"God damn it, Glenn. You had me thinking I was going nuts, and you did it twice. That's real chicken shit."

"I'm sorry, but I couldn't resist it. You looked so damn funny when you first saw Crosby. I just had to do it."

By now we were both laughing.

"Glenn, you're a shit head. Let's go get some coffee."

Crosby knew we were going to fly the mission from here and land at our new field in LeMans, so he said he was going to LeMans and would put on a show for us when we arrived. Arrangements were made in a hurry, and we all gathered in the courtyard to await their transportation. Crosby's party included a comic and two starlets who were absolutely gorgeous, even in their baggy G.I. uniforms. They hugged us and kissed us and said to be careful and they'd see us later in LeMans.

**51**

While we were waiting, the comic told jokes. Crosby talked to us and said he didn't care what the U.S.O. said he was going to LeMans and would definitely do a show for us. The trucks arrived, and they left. I figured that's the last we'd see of them because the U.S.O. people and the army special services sure as hell wouldn't let them put on a show for our small group. They'd have them back on their schedule and shuffled off some place else.

Fred Astaire was on his own. When he found out I was from Los Angeles, he wanted to talk about life in southern California. I had several hours to kill before take-off, so I offered to show him around the area. I was too junior at that time to have my own airplane, but I took him to the one I was going to fly on that mission. I pointed out the machine guns sticking out of the wings and the bombs strapped to the underside. He examined them in awe and was absolutely astounded that he was actually at the scene and talking to the guys who shortly were going out to engage in deadly combat with the Germans. He kept asking, "How can you do this? Aren't you scared?"

"Hell yes, I'm scared, but I was trained for it, consider myself indestructible, am damn good at it, and have a hell of a lot to fight for." He still couldn't get over it; he kept shaking his head, amazed at our attitude.

Our field was close to the area where our gliders landed in the early hours of D-Day morning, so I asked him if he wanted to see it. He did, so we left the perimeter of our airfield, and less than a half a mile away we were examining the remains of the glider fleet. The Germans were aware of our gliders, knew that a great armada of them would be landing at the time of the invasion. As a countermeasure, they put up poles about 15 feet high and thick as fleas all over the area. When our gliders came in for their landing in the dark, they hit the poles, and gliders were strewn all over the place in various degrees of destruction. Some were upside down, wings torn off, front ends smashed; it was a real mess.

We climbed in and around the derelicts. "What about the men in these things. They must have been hurt?" he asked.

"Don't know. It was just like this when we got here, but they must have had plenty of casualties."

He was visibly moved at such destruction. "I've never seen anything like this—never been this close to the war. I'd like to see your plane again."

"Sure, let's go." So we returned to the field and went down the line to my plane. He walked around it, touched it, and I finally said, "Would you like to sit in the cockpit?" He looked at me and said, "I don't deserve to. I could never do what you are doing."

"Horseshit. I think you could if you had to."

He was reluctant, but I had the feeling that he wanted to, so I helped him up, and he climbed in. I hung over the side of the cockpit and pointed out the machine gun trigger and bomb release.

"It's hard to believe I'm really here. You—this airplane—your whole squadron will actually be in combat this afternoon—yet everything seems so normal, so calm; you seem so calm. It's not like I imagined it would be. You have a lot of courage. All you guys do." We headed back to our headquarters.

# CHAPTER 1O: SONG AND DANCE

When we moved to a new field, we had to take a minimum of personal gear with us in the airplane, so I went to pack that, strike my tent, and get it and my sleeping bag back to headquarters for shipment. There was damn little room in the cockpit, but it would hold a shaving kit, and extra clothing could be put on the seat, under your parachute. After I had all that squared away I went back to the ready-room. The mission was still on for 1400 hours.

I had lunch with Astaire, and he said he really should leave, but he was going to wait until after we took off, so we went back to the ready-room, and I invited him to sit in on the briefing. This, of course, was probably against regulations, but I knew no one would be impolite enough to ask him to leave.

When the U.S.O. set up celebrity tours, they were never taken to a combat area. They saw the results of combat when they visited hospitals or old battle fields but were never exposed to the highly charged drama of troops ready to engage in mortal combat.

The atmosphere of a fighter-bomber squadron preparing for battle is deceiving. There are no bombs bursting in air or rockets' red glare. The briefings are more business-like than war-like, even though the subject of killing is predominant. The target is analyzed, and the method of attack discussed. The anticipated flak, weather, evasive action, what to do if you're hit, radio discipline, authenticator code, and a myriad of other problems and procedures are presented to the pilots. Perhaps the greatest drama is when the escape kits are handed out, and each pilot surrenders his wallet and personal belongings to a little cloth bag with his name on it and hopes to hell he'll be alive to retrieve it after the mission. The surroundings are highly charged, but the real essence is subdued. It's there all right, in the casual remarks and bravado conversation, and to an outsider, it must seem like the pilots are not overly concerned, and this will be just a routine ride in the park. But training and self-discipline are now at their highest. It is below the dignity of the pilots to show concern for their personal welfare. The successful execution of the mission is what's important. But the guts are churning, and the slight nausea is there, but that will be overcome.

This is what Fred Astaire experienced. It was totally foreign to him, and there was no way he could understand it. I'm sure that's why he was so awed in our presence. He simply couldn't comprehend our attitude when death may be waiting a short distance away. He stuck around until we took off, but before going out to the planes he stopped me and asked that I please be careful and write to him after this mission was over. He wanted to know if I made it through that mission that he had become such a part of but was afraid to put it in those words.

I did write to him and sent him the pictures I had taken during his visit. He sent back an autographed picture of himself in top hat and tails along with a nice letter inviting me to visit him when I returned home.

I observed a great difference between Crosby and Astaire. Crosby spent most of his time with our senior officers, which included the group commander who had come to the squadron to meet our famous visitors. Crosby wanted the spotlight, had to be the center of attention. I don't mean he wasn't nice. He posed for pictures with us and was very friendly, but there was a certain lack of sincerity.

Fred Astaire was quiet, reserved, content to let Crosby have the spotlight. He was moved by our presence rather than the other way around. His sincerity and humility clearly came through, and he was very pleased to have a 2nd lieutenant rather than a colonel show him around. Years later I heard him described as "The True Gentleman of Hollywood," and indeed, he was.

That mission was an easy one with very little flak. We bombed some gun emplacements, strafed a few trucks, and stayed in the battle area on call for the ground troops until we had to leave. It was dusk when we returned to the new field. As we circled before landing, I saw a very large gathering of troops on the ground and wondered why they were there. We landed and parked the airplanes.

The jeeps picked us up and took us directly to combat operations where the intelligence officer said, "We'll critique later. You're going right to the show. There are 5,000 troops waiting, but Crosby won't start till you guys get there." We pulled up in back of the crowd; there was an open aisle to the stage. Everyone was sitting on the ground, but in front of the stage were 12 chairs—just for us. Crosby, the girls, and the comic greeted us, and the girls hugged us and cried with happiness that we had all come back. Then the comic announced from the stage that we had returned and the show started.

Incidents such as this fed the ego of the Thunderbolt pilot. He knew he was somebody and that the front-line troops depended on him, and he wanted that recognition from everyone. He knew he was courageous and basked in self-glory when others told him so. He was the guy with the guts—the guy who could look death in the face and say, "Fuck you."

I personally was very touched by this event. It made me realize that people at home were very aware of what we were doing; they worried about us; they prayed for us; they appreciated beyond words what we were doing. We were taking the brunt of it, paying the price, but they didn't consider us suckers or jerks for risking our lives; they were in back of us 100 percent. It was their war, too.

# CHAPTER 10: SONG AND DANCE

Crosby had also become part of that mission and in his own way responded the best he knew how to. He kept his word. He put on a show just for us. The fact that 5,000 others were present was incidental in his mind and that of the girls and the comic.

After the show we said good-bye to our famous guests and went back to combat operations; we still had to critique the mission. With that over we went to our new quarters and started to get settled in. There were five of us—the fearless five—in the tent, the same set up we had at the old field except our cots were not in the same positions they had been in in relationship to the tent flap, which was the entrance to the tent. This later proved to be very significant.

Three of the guys had moved a couple of days ahead of my buddy Jim and me and had scouted the area to find an alternate booze supply in the unfortunate event that ours was delayed or lost in the move.

They came up with something new to us called Calvados and said we wouldn't be able to drink three shots of it and stay on our feet. We immediately accepted the challenge, drank three shots, and passed out. In self-defense I'll add that it was a very large shot glass. But that was not the end of the activities.

At about 0300 hours one of the guys woke up and had to go; his cot had formerly faced the tent opening. He got out of bed and headed for the tent opening, but due to the changed floor plan, the tent opening was now to his left and another cot faced his; he was still too zonked to know the difference and started to pee.

All hell broke loose. The guy being peed on started yelling and cursing, and we all woke up; someone turned on the light, and we saw one guy struggling to get out of his sleeping bag while the other guy was peeing all over him.

The three of us not involved in this minor catastrophe started to laugh and laughed so hard we nearly cried. Needless to say, they changed sleeping bags and cots immediately, and after apologies and more laughing on our part, we finally settled down and went back to sleep. It had been quite a day.

## chapter 11

# THE RABBIT AND THE TIGER

**I**s courage something that's always there way down deep in one's personality and only activated in the presence of extreme events? If a person performs a courageous act once, does that mean he will always be courageous, or is it something that may only happen once in a lifetime? From my personal experience, courage seems to be a reaction—not an action—to events that transpire. It's part of a person's psyche and under the right circumstances will become their normal and natural action. But everything must be just right, all the neurotransmitters working in the proper sequence, the sights, the smells, everything in its proper order; the event must be powerful enough to set this energy into an irreversible countdown. It's what makes one man a hero and another a coward.

We had one flight leader who most of us considered a rabbit. He would attack the target assigned but wouldn't go back in to shoot up the flak guns or anything that might be spotted that should also have been hit. He did what he was ordered to do and nothing more. I flew with him a few times and didn't like it. A fighter-bomber pilot should be aggressive. He's trained to attack; that's why he's there. The rabbit was one of the "Old Boys," so nothing was ever said about his milquetoast approach to combat flying. He was very mild mannered, rarely drank, didn't smoke, and never spoke up at a squadron meeting; however, he handled the P-47 well and was easy to fly with as far as formation was concerned. We had no other words to describe him except chicken shit. That all changed one day in September.

The squadron had returned from its mission, and the pilots were back in the tent area, officers' row, when one of the guys who'd flown that mission yelled over to me.

"Hey, Glenn, come here. You'll want to hear this."

It was hot that afternoon, and several of the guys had gathered at one tent—several of the new boys that is. The tent flaps were up to try to catch what little breeze there was. I went in and sat on a cot.

"What's up?" I asked.

Herb, who had been on the mission, started his story. "Wait till you hear this. You know old chicken shit, the rabbit. Well he's a rabbit no more; now he's a tiger." We, of course, thought he was kidding.

# CHAPTER 11: THE RABBIT AND THE TIGER

"That bastard has guts," he continued. "We were on our way back, about 2,500 feet and damn near in friendly territory when a quadmount 20 opened up and drilled Eddie right through the canopy. The rabbit, I mean the tiger, had just looked over to check—you know how he always checks to see that you're in position—when this quadmount opened up, and he saw Eddie's head explode. Eddie went straight in. Anyway, the old man ordered an immediate attack, but the tiger came on the radio, told everyone to hold their position, pulled off, and went straight in for that 20."

"All by himself?"

"You're damn right. He went straight for him. The guy was in a clearing, and we could see everything. Anyway, he didn't nail him, and as he pulled away, that Heini gunner was right on his tail. The old man called for another attack, but the tiger came back on the radio and said, 'No!—told everyone to hold their position.' By that time our flight is out a ways, and I can't see what's going on."

Another guy finished the story. "I did. That bastard swung his gun around in my direction, and I figured if he fired, I was going after him, but here comes the tiger about 300 feet with black smoke pouring out. He must of been on emergency power and water injection. Anyway, the gunner turned toward him and started to fire, and the tiger started to fire. Christ, he must of closed to 50 feet. I thought he was going to crash right into that fucking gun."

"And get this—nobody has said a God damn word over the radio. We're just all circling and watching. So when he pulls over the gun, it ain't shootin' no more. But the tiger does a sharp wingover and goes at him again—still shootin' like a son-of-a-bitch. When he pulls off this time, the gun is shot and the crew creamed."

Herb finished the story. "Then he pulls up into formation, tells his flight to close in, and the old man heads for home."

I was absolutely flabbergasted at this story.

"My God," I asked, "what did he say about it at critique?"

"Not a God damn thing. When we were reporting our claims, he just said, 'I destroyed a quadmount 20 and the crew.' That's all he said, except he did say he saw Eddie's head explode."

Someone in the corner said, "What ever possessed him to do that?"

Herb answered him. "I don't know? I always thought he was a chicken shit, but that bastard's got more guts than I have."

At dinner that night everyone was telling him what a fantastic thing he had done. He was quite reserved about the entire affair and made very little comment on it. The next mission he flew he was his old cautious, conservative self, but the term chicken shit, or rabbit, was never used again. From then on we openly called him tiger. He didn't seem to mind.

But what of the other side of the coin? When personal honor is thrown to the wind? When duty is not strong enough to conquer fear? Is it deep in the genes like a mutated cell waiting to break forth and dominate one's personality? Again, I believe it's a reaction, brought about when a given number of circumstances occur at a precise time and place, the coalescence of which is so powerful as to overcome all other emotions and results in cowardice.

Who knows the answer to this? But I have seen examples of both. We share in the glory of the hero but withdraw in the presence of the coward.

The selection process for fighter-bomber combat pilots was exhaustive. After that long process you would expect the final product would be perfect. Well, it was nearly so. Very few pilots were busted out of combat squadron, but there were some. I remember when several came to us as replacements. There were three of them. Two had been buddies all through school; the third, they had just met at the replacement pool. It was dark when they arrived and cold; they were looking for a bunk. We were living in tents and were to move to a more forward position in a day or two. Fortunately we ended up at a nice field near Rheims, France. This actually was the first time we'd ever been stationed at a place where they had buildings and a black-top runway. It was an honest-to-God airfield formerly occupied by the Luftwaffe. Once we got squared away these new boys would begin flying combat missions. The two buddies wanted to be in the same flight, but that was not possible. One was assigned to Jim's flight and one to mine. Jim and I were element leaders at the time. The respective flight leaders, being still part of the "Old Boys" clique, took little interest in their new pilots, but Jim and I, remembering how it was when we were new replacements, invited them to our room for a booze and bull session. We went over the latest combat tactics, explained how we made an attack and how we aimed our bombs. I remember especially cautioning them on the extra load they would be carrying, which gave the plane a different feeling. In stateside training they only had four machine guns on board and no bombs or external gas tanks. On a combat mission you took off with eight guns, a full load of ammunition, two 500-pound bombs, and an extra 150 gallons of gas in an external tank. This was an added weight of over a ton, and you had to handle the plane accordingly to prevent a stall.

It was standard procedure for the operations officer to check out all new pilots. The next day he picked the one in Jim's flight, and they went up for a short ride. The planes were equipped with wing tanks, and they were full, adding about 1,500 pounds above what the new guy was used to.

The landing pattern placed the approach right over our quarters, and as he made his final turn, he got too slow, stalled out, and crashed. It was a miracle he didn't explode and burn. We all ran over to the crash site intending to pull him out of the plane. What we found was a guy in perfect shape from the shoulders down but nothing but a bloody pulp for a head. His buddy really came apart at the sight.

The operations officer checked him out the next day, on a short flight, and he seemed to do okay, so he was put on schedule for the next mission. He was the one who was in my flight, but I didn't fly that mission. Here is what happened.

When the squadron reached the target, the squadron leader made his attack so that the pullout would be into the sun. This new guy was flying wing to the last flight leader. There was some flak, but it was not too bad. The first two flights went in, and then his flight leader rolled over and started down, but he wouldn't go. The element leader finally left him up there and dove on the target with his wing man. He was ordered again to attack the target, but he refused. He was so petrified he was barely able to fly home. This had never happened before in our squadron, and I don't think anyone knew how to handle it. We all felt sorry for him because of his buddy's death and the fact that he had seen the body in such a mutilated condition, but that didn't alter the fact that he was supposed to be a combat pilot, which meant you could take anything that was dished out.

Everyone avoided him at mess, and after dinner I took a bottle of whiskey and went to his quarters to find out what went wrong. He was sitting on his bunk crying, which was something else that had never happened in our squadron.

I looked at this guy; he was a big blond kid with a chubby face. He didn't even look like a pilot—let alone a Thunderbolt pilot. Had he slipped through the cracks? But looks can be deceiving; remember the rabbit that turned into a tiger. Even though he royally screwed up today, he deserves another chance.

"Ned," I began, "I want to know what went wrong today, and for Christ's sake quit crying. You're in my flight. I want to help you if I can.

"So okay, what happened?"

"I don't know."

"You were the one in the cockpit. Why didn't you follow your leader down and bomb?"

"Well—I watched the first flight go in, and every one of them crashed and exploded—and the same thing happened to the next flight. When my flight leader rolled over to go down, I just couldn't go." And then very quietly he said, "I didn't want to die."

I thought about this for awhile and finally realized what had happened.

"Ned," I began, "you saw bombs exploding not airplanes crashing."

"But nobody pulled away from the target; they all went in—or at least I thought they did."

"The squadron leader called you on the radio, ordered you to attack the target. How could he do that if he had crashed?"

"I don't know. I was so scared. I was shaking and sick to my stomach. It was all I could do to fly the plane. It was terrible."

I had a drink from the bottle I brought with me, offered him one, and he took a sip. What the hell was I going to tell this guy?

"Listen to me, Ned. Are you willing to go on another combat mission?"

After an uncomfortable silence he said, "I'd like to try, but I'm scared."

He was looking directly at me, pleading for understanding and compassion, and suddenly I realized he just didn't understand the situation he was in. I began softly but firmly.

"Ned, we're all scared. Every pilot in this squadron and every other squadron over here is scared. I've seen guys turn white at briefing when a particularly tough target was announced. Sometimes flying through a flak barrage I've been so scared I've almost puked in my oxygen mask. But you've got to overcome it."

We sat in silence for awhile. Finally he said, "I just don't want to die."

"I've never met a fighter-bomber pilot who did, but you may as well face the fact that you might."

After another prolonged silence he looked at me again and asked, "How do you face it?" I think my answer surprised him.

"I do what I have to do. At first I thought I was so God damn good that no German son of a bitch could lay a hand on me. After I got shot down I realized they could, but I survived and still felt I was indestructible. After a few more missions I realized I wasn't. Believe me, it gets tougher and tougher as time goes on and more of your friends get killed. But you owe a duty to your country. If we lose the war, we lose everything. I'm willing to lose my life for that cause and so are the rest of the guys; just keep thinking that way. Tell yourself you're brave; tell yourself you're a God damn hero; sing the air corps song to yourself. Look at the other guys; they're as scared as you are, but they still climb into the cockpit and dive on the target. If they can do it, you can do it. And remember you're not alone. We're all in the same boat. And you see this bottle here—it's the best friend you've got."

We sat there awhile, and finally he said, "Okay, I'll try."

"All right. Tell you what, I'm not on tomorrow's schedule, but I will be on the next. I'll ask the operations officer to put you on my wing—okay?"

"Yes, thanks."

"Now let me tell you something. I want you on my wing like glue. When I roll over, you roll over with me. You stay right there—right on my wing. Don't look at the target; look at me. When you see my bomb drop, you drop yours. Don't pay any attention to the flak. I'll dodge it for both of us. But God damn it, you stick with me all the way in and all the way out—okay?"

"Okay," he answered.

"Get some sleep. I'm gonna get drunk." And as an after thought I added, "You aughta try it. It helps."

The next day I interceded with the squadron commander, and he agreed to give him another chance. My flight leader was not happy with my Dear Abby role, but two days later we went. I was leading the element, and he flew my wing. When we attacked the target, instead of following me in to the deck to bomb, he released about 3,000 feet in the air and pulled away; naturally he missed the target by a mile. Well, that was it as far as I was concerned. He just didn't have the right stuff. The next day he was relieved from duty and sent away; I have no idea what finally happened to him. After over a year of intensive training and passing the selection process time after time, when it came to the final moment of truth, he was found lacking. The process wasn't 100 percent perfect. Was it that he had no courage, could not muster the chemical burst necessary to excite the neurotransmitters into action? What makes one man a coward and another a hero?

## chapter 12

# LUCK OR ?

How much did luck have to do with survival? Well it had a great deal to do with it, but, in the long run, barring a stroke of fate, skill and the survival instinct were more important—statistically, that is. Let me relate an incident and you be the judge.

In early July, when the squadron was flying from England, a group mission was called to attack a railroad marshaling yard west of Paris. The group, on the way to the target, passed north of Rouen, France. Rouen was noted for intense, accurate flak, and the flight path was planned to miss most of it.

Things were progressing satisfactorily, landfall-in—that means reaching the French coast after crossing the English Channel—was made precisely where it was supposed to be made and on time. No flak was encountered up to this point. Each squadron was spread out in proper battle formation, and things were uneventful. Suddenly a cluster burst of flak bracketed one of the squadrons. One plane received a direct hit and exploded in a huge fireball. The pilot must have been killed instantly. No other planes received any damage, and that was the only burst of flak fired. It was his fourth mission.

Could you shrug this off as an unlucky hit, the luck of the draw? There seems no other explanation. He was exactly where he was supposed to be in a formation of 36 airplanes, yet he was instantly killed, and no one else received so much as a scratch on the skin of his plane.

Most squadrons had what was called a "mission board" that hung on the wall in operations. This board listed every pilot chronologically that had ever been a member of the squadron during its combat operations. It also listed the number of missions flown and the type of mission. It was set up in block-graph form. At a glance you could see each pilot's record stacked up against every other member of the squadron. At the extreme right side of the graph was a blank space, and when a pilot was shot down, an hourglass with the sand at the bottom was placed in this space indicating his time had run out.

There was practically a straight line, from top to bottom, which varied between the third and fifth mission. It seemed, if the pilot could get by the fifth mission, he had gained enough survival experience to improve his chances of living for awhile.

From the fifth on there was no statistical significance as to the number of missions flown, except, as the numbers increased, there were more and more hourglasses on the right side of the chart.

Getting back to the pilot who was blown to smithereens by that direct hit near Rouen—was it pure bad luck?

When we first arrived in France, our airfield was in the Cherbourg area in the middle of an old apple orchard. We weren't alone in that area. There were more than a half dozen similar fields within five-minutes flying time of where we were located.

These were temporary fields made by placing layers of tar paper over the dirt. Actually they weren't too bad, except they were short. Someone, somewhere had told the invasion planners that a P-47 Thunderbolt required 3,800 feet to land, so naturally the field was built to that dimension.

That would have been okay, as far as it went, but sometimes it took more than 3,800 feet to take off. We were faced with a problem and no immediate answer. Our only recourse was to take off anyway and hope we would make it.

Now, landing in 3,800 feet was possible under ideal conditions, but if you were nursing a sick airplane or a little discombobulated from being shot at, you had no margin of safety at all.

To protect the field from German night fighters, some antiaircraft guns were installed. The idiot in charge of that put a big 90-millimeter gun at the end of the runway. So not only were we flying out of a dangerously short field but we had to hurdle that gun just as our wheels were leaving the ground. We complained, but it didn't do any good.

On the afternoon of the fourth day the squadron took off on a mission. Each plane was loaded with two 500-pound wing bombs; it was hot, and there was no wind. Eleven planes made it off, but one did not. He was going full bore down the runway but just couldn't lift it off the ground and crashed into that gun. Fortunately his bombs didn't go off, but there was gasoline all over the place, and an explosion was expected imminently. The ground crews, disregarding their own safety, rushed to the crashed airplane and desperately tried to get the pilot out. He was trapped in the wreckage; someone brought an ax and cut away at the canopy to try to free him. He finally was pulled out but was badly mangled—his head nearly cut off. It could have been from the ax. I don't think anyone really knew or wanted to know. The pilot was taken to the dispensary and a call went out for blood. The whole squadron lined up to give, but it was too late. The flight surgeon pronounced him dead.

As far as the rest of the pilots were concerned, that was it—lengthen the runway, get the gun out of the way, or get somebody else to fly the missions. By the end of the next day the mangled gun was removed, and the engineers had bulldozed an additional 500 feet of clear space at the end of the runway. They also cleared an additional 500 feet on the landing end. It was still tight at times, when the air was hot and heavy and there was no head wind, but we managed to fly out of there for several more weeks, until we were moved farther into central France, without any more accidents.

# CHAPTER 12: LUCK OR ?

How did luck fit into this situation? The pilot was experienced, probably had flown 20 missions by that time, so he was used to taking off a fully combat-loaded P-47—in fact, it was his own airplane. Eleven other planes made it off safely. What happened? He was never able to tell us, so we'll never know; just chalk it up to bad luck.

We had just pulled off the target and were climbing to get out of flak range and reassemble the squadron when one of the flight leaders called.

"This is Blue leader. I've got a 40 millimeter in my cockpit."

"This is Bonebreak leader. Say again, Blue leader."

"I've got a 40-millimeter shell through the bottom of the floor, and gas is sloshing into the cockpit."

Someone cut in, "Get out of that thing before it blows."

"Bonebreak Blue leader, this is Bonebreak leader. You are 20 minutes from friendly territory. Do you want to bail out? That shell is probably a dud."

"I'll stick with it for a while."

Another unidentified voice came on the radio.

"Blue leader, it could be a delayed fuse."

I'm sure the caller was trying to be helpful, but the squadron leader didn't take it that way.

"Bonebreak squadron from Bonebreak leader. I'll have no more unidentified radio transmission. Blue leader, they do not use time delayed fuses in antiaircraft shells; it's obviously a dud."

"Roger, Bonebreak leader. I think you're right, but I have gas all over the floor."

"Blue leader from Bonebreak leader. I suggest you bail out as soon as we get over friendly territory."

"Roger, Bonebreak leader."

Twenty minutes came and went, and the shell had not exploded. We were now over our own lines, and he could bail out any time he chose to. More minutes ticked by, and we were all sweating it out with him, imagining ourselves in his predicament. He finally decided he'd stay with it and land at the home field. Actually, we had a good field at that time, about a 6,000-foot runway of smooth blacktop. Now the squadron leader was faced with a problem. Could he allow that plane to land and possibly, if it blew up on landing, jeopardize the lives of other personnel and equipment. He suggested, not ordered, him to bail out, but the flight leader told him he'd rather take a chance on landing than risk a bailout.

So the stage was set. We all landed and parked our planes in their regular places; he was told that after landing he was to taxi to the corner of the field, way out by himself and get away from the plane as fast as he could. And that's just exactly what happened. The landing went off without a hitch. He saved himself and the airplane. He was not an exceptional pilot, just average, so it wasn't superior flying skill that brought him through—if not that—Luck?

## chapter 13

# REALITY

While we were training in the States, we naturally assumed our combat assignments would be with the Eighth Fighter Command. As far as we knew, that was the only Air Force in Europe. A new instructor pilot appeared one day; he was a big guy, a captain, handsome, with a handlebar mustache and a chest full of ribbons. But what made him intriguing was that he had just completed a tour of duty in the Eighth Air Force, flying Thunderbolts. We found him that night in the officers' club, sitting by himself at the bar. This was too good an opportunity to pass up. None of us had ever met a combat pilot before.

"Hi, Captain. Are you gonna be our instructor?"

He introduced himself, and we joined him without invitation and ordered drinks.

"Well," he began, "that's what I'm supposed to be, but so far I haven't been told exactly what to do. Are you guys flying the Thunderbolt?"

"Yes, sir. We've been here for two months, have over a 100 hours in the Jug." (The Jug was a nickname for the P-47.)

"Then by now you should be able to handle it."

"Well a little at least. You flew with the Eighth—right?"

"Yah, for a year, escorting B-17s."

"Did you get in lots of dogfights?"

"Yah."

"What's it like?"

"It's fast. Sometimes a fight doesn't last more than 30 seconds. Everyone gets spread out all over the sky, and no matter how high you start, the God damn dogfight always ends up under 10,000 feet."

There was a pause as we assimilated this. We had been led to believe you always stayed at the altitude of the bombers.

"But aren't you supposed to stay with the bombers?"

"Yes and no. You're supposed to protect the bombers, so when you tangle with enemy fighters, you try and stay with them until you shoot 'em down or they run, then you rejoin the bombers."

"What do you do if one gets on your ass?"

# CHAPTER 13: REALITY

He thought a moment before answering. I believe he realized this was a time for pure truth. His accurate advice was essential to our survival.

"Well, first off, you keep your head constantly turning, so if someone begins to get on your ass, you know it. Then you tell your wing man to cover your ass. He's the bait. They're supposed to get on his ass, then you move over and shoot 'em down."

"Christ, that's kind of hard on wing men," somebody said.

"Not if you both know what you're doing. And remember the Thunderbolt's the fastest son of a bitch in the world going straight down. No German fighter can stay with you, so if you're in trouble, you usually can dive out of it."

We ordered more drinks, and now there were several other guys crowded around listening. We kept this question and answer game up for several nights running. One night I asked him, "What are living conditions like in England? Were your quarters okay? Food? Did you have a decent 'O' club?"

"Oh, shit," he warmed to this question, "you'll love it. I lived in a big Tudor mansion—like a semi-castle. There were 12 of us there. Had a private room, a bat man . . ."

"Bat man, what's that?" somebody asked.

"He's an orderly, keeps your stuff in shape, cleans your room, sees to your laundry—all that stuff. Two A.T.S. girls served breakfast. There was a lounge, bar, and dining room on the main floor. It was great."

"The airdrome was about two miles away. We bicycled back and forth but had jeeps if we went into town."

"How about women? Were there lots around?"

"Lots! Jesus you had your pick. They flocked to the club, and nobody said anything if they stayed all night.

"The weather's bad, worst flying conditions in the whole world, but other than that, it was perfect. You'll love London, more pussy than you can imagine."

This guy was a hero to us; he'd been there; he'd shot down German fighters, became an ace, and had survived. We couldn't wait to get to England and get in the war ourselves.

Although we never found our semi-castle or the rest of the life he described, we did accomplish our main objective and that was to fly the Thunderbolt in combat.

After we arrived and were assigned to the Ninth Air Force, our disappointment was keen. We had been handed a double whammy. First off, our chances of survival had been reduced to less than half, and the possibility of ever becoming an ace was nonexistent. But that's the way it is in a war; you play with the cards you're dealt; you obey orders and do the best job you can do. So now you had one thought only—become the best fighter-bomber pilot in the war.

Once we joined our squadrons we found the pilot's only duty was to fly combat missions, and those averaged about 10 a month. We had plenty of time on our hands, and that was used up in letter writing, bull sessions, and wandering around the field looking at the planes. When a plane came back shot up, we would examine it closely and ask the pilot how it handled and what trouble he encountered in getting it home. It was a confidence builder to see a very badly mauled Thunderbolt and know that the pilot had been able to bring it back and live to fly another day.

We usually had a record player and a small but precious supply of records. Those old 78s were brittle and highly subject to scratching, but they were played over and over again; the quality diminished as the war progressed.

When a mission was out, those left behind were uneasy until the squadron returned. Although, as I have said earlier, everyone didn't love everyone else, the overall concern for the squadron was still there. You worried about your close friends because, as they were individually killed off, your burden of survival became greater. You couldn't help but think, "He was a damn good pilot. If he could get shot down, so could I."

In the ground forces, the higher the commander, the farther he was from the front lines where the killing was going on. In an air force unit it was a different matter. The squadron commander flew as many missions as any pilot in the outfit. The group commander did the same, and when there was no target worthy of a group mission, he would often fly with one of the squadrons. Their casualty rate was high. In my squadron we had three commanders during the year of combat flying: two of the three were killed. There was no such thing as a safe position. There was, however, one that was definitely unsafe, the most vulnerable in the flight, and that was Blue four—the last man in the formation—tail-end Charlie. It was also a very important position because enemy fighters always jumped the squadron from the rear, so it was Blue four's job to protect the squadron from a surprise attack. During dive-bombing and strafing runs he was the last man into the target. By that time the flak gunners had perfected their range and approach angle, so their shooting was more accurate. But it is possible to defy the odds. I personally flew 20 missions as Blue four and survived. I actually got to enjoy the responsibility of the position.

Over the years I've talked to many of the old Fighter-Bomber Boys. My impression is that the groups were all very much alike. Each had its share of excellent pilots, good pilots, and passable pilots. The vast majority were single; wives were an unnecessary burden. Everyone, however, had a girlfriend, or more than one, and the conversation would always end up about sex, after talking about flying and how the Thunderbolt was the best airplane for combat ever built.

Although the personality profiles of the fighter-bomber pilots were similar, as individuals they were a diverse lot. In my squadron we had two Jewish guys, one American Indian, two Germans, and an Italian—whose mother regularly sent him salami that smelled so bad we made him hang it in a tree away from our tent—plus a mix of other nationalities most generally referred to as Anglo-Saxons. There was never a racial slur or snide remark about those who were not blue-eyed or light-haired. Each man earned the respect of the others based on his abilities as a combat pilot.

# PHOTO GALLERY

Cadets worked hard to graduate as single-engine fighter pilots; however, it was a difficult journey from the AT-6 trainer to a P-47 Thunderbolt.

The author's plane was reassigned from the Eighth Air Force to the Ninth Air Force when the Eighth changed over to P-51s.

The fighter-bomber pilots often lived under the same conditions as infantry soldiers.

67

The Officers' Mess. Not only could the fighter-bomber pilots handle their P-47 Thunderbolts, but when necessary, could cook their own meals.

Ground crews were dedicated to maintaining their airplanes in top condition, fully capable for combat operations. This group belies the usual look of mud, fatigue, and lack of sleep which was the norm. *Charles Queen*

Author astride a 1,000-pound bomb.

Major repair work was done by specialized crews. Early on, the hangars were tents; later, they were part of captured Luftwaffe bases. *Charles Queen*

Author's passport photos used in the escape kit that each fighter-bomber pilot carried while flying missions over France and Belgium. However, the Germans weren't fooled.

Informal briefing. Note facial expressions of anxiety, anticipation, and fear. The thought is always present at this time—is this the day I die? *Charles Queen*

The author's P-47 Thunderbolt. Note the modified bubble (Malcomb) canopy.

Briefings conducted later in the war were in facilities formerly occupied by Luftwaffe pilots. Note the aircraft silhouettes on the left. Upper row are the German jets, the ME 262 and 163. *Charles Queen*

The bridge over the Loire River at Tours, France. This and other bridges were attacked and destroyed by P-47 Thunderbolts and medium bombers of the Ninth Air Force.

Heading for the Battle of the Bulge. Enemy forces were very near the fighter-bomber bases in Belgium, so belly tanks were not needed. Note crew chiefs riding the right wing to direct pilots on narrow taxiways. *Peter Coccio*

Landing a battle-damaged plane was dangerous and not always successful. *Charles Queen*

The only "good" 88 is a "dead" 88.

When we saw this big German 88 antiaircraft gun and the size of the shells they were shooting at us, we realized why the 88 had attained the reputation as a plane killer.

The dreaded German quadmount 20-millimeter antiaircraft gun. More fighter-
bombers were lost to this weapon than any other.

P-47 Thunderbolt fighter-bombers attacked Luftwaffe bases. Infantry and armored divisions captured them, and then they were ours.

Wreckage of the Author's Thunderbolt 6V. Battle damage occurred while dive bombing in Nantes, France. Glenn nursed the plane back to the crash site near Dover, England.

Author ready to fly. Note first-aid kit attached to the parachute harness (right side). The kit contained a Syrette (shot) of morphine to help bear the pain if wounded. Plugs in machine gun barrels meant the plane had been fueled, armed, and was ready to go.

Bing Crosby with author.

Author with two starlets from Bing Crosby's U.S.O. tour group.

Six new eager 2nd lieutenant replacement pilots anxious for combat assignment.

Quite a stag line.

# chapter 14
# COME FLY WITH ME

What's it like to fly in combat? It's been said many times that combat flying cannot be described: you have to experience it to know what it's like.

I'm going to try to overcome that truism by inviting you to join me. The Thunderbolt is a single-seat airplane. Maybe your body can't come with me, but your mind can, and that's the part of you that experiences emotion, stress, and memory.

We, that's you and I, will be together during the entire happening. We'll meet in the ready-room this morning, sit through briefing, fly the mission, critique when we return, and get drunk together tonight when we talk out the details of how the mission went with our other pilot friends.

I can tell you now it will be a typical fighter-bomber mission in support of General Patton's Third Army as he pushes across central France in August of 1944.

It's 1000 hours. We're on standby, so we have to be in the ready-room. If we have to go to the can, we check out with the operations officer; he'll keep a clerk standing by to run and get us if the mission is called. The only one free to leave is the squadron commander who spends most of his time between the ready-room and combat operations. We'll be flying Blue three position; that's element leader in the last flight. We'll be the second to last man to attack the target, if we all go in on the same target. Otherwise, our flight will get a target of its own.

We've got everything with us that we can take. There's no prescribed uniform. We can wear whatever we like. But we're wearing G.I. shoes, in case we have to "walk" out. It's summer and hot, but we've still got pants and shirt on under our flying suit plus our leather jacket. We'll sweat in the cockpit, but if shot down, we'll have a jacket tonight when it's cold and we're under a bush hiding from Germans and hoping to make contact with the French underground who can rescue us and get us back to our own lines.

We're carrying a 45-caliber automatic pistol in a shoulder holster; a hunting knife is strapped to our leg, and the escape kit is zipped into the shin pocket of our flying suit. We've got our good luck charm in our pants pocket; we absolutely won't fly without it.

Although our escape kits have a two-day supply of food, we've got an extra "D" ration, extra cigarettes everywhere we can stash them, and our Zippo lighter is freshly filled.

Nothing is happening. We smoke, drink coffee, and shoot the breeze with the other guys. Sometimes the flight surgeon or the intelligence officer drops in, and we talk with them for awhile. If there's anything new on the French underground or escape techniques, we find out about it. But if you're not feeling up to par, don't even hint about it to the flight surgeon. He can pull a pilot off the schedule in the blink of an eye. He has the authority to ground any pilot, including the squadron commander. The padre is around but inconspicuous; if you need him, he's here to help. The time really drags; that doesn't do our nerves any good.

We go to lunch early, all of us together. We're served first. We eat in a hurry and go back to the ready-room together. When we get back, we find the squadron has been moved from standby to immediate alert. Something must be happening.

Finally at 1400 hours the squadron commander comes in joined by the operations officer. We've been through this plenty of times before, but still our guts are going to churn, our heart thumps, and we have a slight sour feeling in our stomach; this is something a pilot will never get used to. We light a cigarette to help settle down.

No elaborate briefing here; no big spotlights glaring on a wall-size map in a gymnasium-size room; no raised platform with tables occupied by helpful staff officers. It's just 15 guys standing around in a tent with a dirt floor, looking at a map pinned to a temporary holder against the tent wall. The extra people are the operations officer, who is a pilot and flies missions but is not flying this one, the intelligence officer, not a pilot, who'll tell us what flak to expect, and the infantry liaison officer. The operations officer begins the briefing.

"There's six heavy artillery pieces dug in and revetted here," he points to the X on the map. "That's eight miles behind the front. They are your primary targets. After you finish them off, you'll work with forward ground control. If they don't have any targets for you within 15 minutes, you're released to look for targets of opportunity; there should be plenty of them in the area. Your ground controller will be Prairie Dog."

The intelligence officer takes over and begins by giving the authenticator for the mission, then continues, "We don't know what the flak situation will be at the target, but expect those guns to be heavily defended; if they're dug in and revetted, it means they plan on staying for awhile. There'll be support personnel, so look for them bivouacked in the surrounding area."

Now we all turn to the infantry liaison officer; he knows what it's like on the ground.

"Gentlemen," he begins, "those long range guns are raising hell with our troops. They can cut a company of infantry to pieces in short order, and that's just what they're doing; casualties have been heavy. I can't stress enough the importance of knocking them out. You've got a lot of guys down there depending on you."

Things are very quiet. He really lays it on you. If you don't get those guns, our guys will continue to be blown apart and die. It's up to you. We feel good now, no sour stomach; we can't wait to get going.

**84**

The squadron commander looks everyone over. "We're armed with 500-pound wing bombs—instantaneous fuses. We'll also be carrying a belly tank. We'll go in at 10,000 feet. When we get to the target, I'll circle it until everyone in my flight picks out a gun. Call your target. I don't want two planes going after one gun. When we're ready, we'll go in. Yellow flight, you wait until we bomb. If there's only two guns left, Yellow three and four will look for something else, but don't pick a target to bomb that you can destroy with machine gun fire."

"Blue flight, you give us top cover, but if we miss, then you finish off what's left. Our job is to silence those guns—period."

"We may catch a lot of flak at the target, especially Blue flight. Take what evasive action you can, but keep us in sight and covered. After we bomb, if there's anything left, we'll strafe."

He gives us a brief looking over and says, "Let's go. G.I.s are dying out there."

The jeeps are waiting and take us to the equipment tent by the flight line. We get our parachutes and helmets. Our goggles and oxygen mask with built-in microphone and headset are attached to our helmet, but we check them anyway, as well as the extra knife that's attached to the chest straps of our chute. If you float down into a tree, you may have to cut yourself free; if you're hurt, you may not be able to get to your leg knife. We put our chute on and head for the jeep; it takes us to our plane.

We greet the crew chief with a casual salute, "Everything okay, Chief?"

"Everything's fine, sir. No problems. It's set to go." We grasp the handhold, put our foot in the toe hold, and start to pull ourselfs up onto the wing. He pushes on our ass, and we finally make it. The Thunderbolt is big. It's an effort to get into the cockpit. Once we're in he helps with the seatbelt and shoulder harness; his assistant on the other side checks our parachute straps, and we're ready.

Sometimes there's confusion at this point. In a formal briefing for a preselected target with a known time of takeoff, you are given a start-engine-time and a begin-to-taxi time, but on this type of scramble mission we'll either get it by radio, ground signal, or we'll just figure it out ourselfs. We turn the radio on and listen. Very shortly we hear, "Bonebreak squadron from Bonebreak leader—start your engines." We don't start immediately. We're number 11, so we watch the other planes. When our flight leader starts, we start. Once the engine is running the crew chief will lie down on the wing and wrap one arm around the machine gun so that he can hold on. The other arm will be used to signal directions to us as we taxi. The Thunderbolt has a tail wheel, so the rear end is low and the front end high; while we're on the ground, we have no forward vision. So the crew chief becomes our forward vision with arm signals.

Once in the takeoff area he tosses us a salute and hops off; the assistant launch officer will guide us into line for takeoff.

Now we run up the engine, check the mags, bring the throttle back to fast idle, push the flap control to full flaps, double check our harness, lock it into takeoff position, and check the canopy—open and locked. It's noisy, exciting, and controlled confusion. Our eyes are on the launch officer now; we're next in line. When he drops the flag for the plane ahead of us, we'll release the brakes, roll into takeoff position, apply full brakes, lock the tail wheel, and watch the flag. He begins to wave it in small circles, slowly at first, and we apply throttle. He continues the circles, but now they're getting bigger and faster as his arm raises. We apply steady throttle pressure and match his rhythm. We better be at full throttle when his arm is fully raised because that's when he brings the flag down sharply and we release the brakes.

We've been holding the stick back in our guts and standing on the brakes. The plane is shaking violently ready to leap into the air; the noise is deafening, the vibration painful. We're at full throttle—2,300 horses raring to go. It's the excitement of takeoff, and the adrenaline is flowing; our legs are trembling, our mouth is dry, and our guts are churning. Down comes the flag, and we release the brakes, but the plane doesn't leap into the air. It begins a slow acceleration down the runway. We can't see ahead of us. At 70 miles per hour the tail feels light, and forward pressure on the stick brings it up. Give it right rudder; fight the torque as it builds. Now things are better; we can see down the runway and feel the wind in our face. We're at 90 miles per hour; acceleration is increasing—100—105  110. The airplane still feels heavy; the Thunderbolt has no inclination to fly itself off the ground—120—130. We're still gaining speed but running out of runway. Pull it off the ground; it won't fly itself off. Now! Back on the stick, and we feel it claw the air; it's a little wobbly but getting better. Up with the gear; now things are smoother—180. Milk up the flaps, close the canopy, check the temperature gauge, close the cowl flaps. We're at 200 miles per hour and 100 feet in the air. We start our turn to join the formation; adjust the throttle, mixture control, and prop pitch for climbing; unlock our shoulder harness; and slide into formation. Our wing man soon joins us. All 12 planes are now in formation on a steady climbing course to 10,000 feet. We can relax a bit now. Suddenly we realize our mouth is not dry, our legs aren't shaking, and our guts are calm; we feel great. It's 40 minutes to the target. We're climbing at 500 feet a minute. That rate of climb will give us maximum forward motion to altitude gained, and in 20 minutes the squadron levels out at 10,000 feet. We look around.

The Thunderbolt isn't sleek, especially when slung with wing bombs and a belly tank. It doesn't have the pleasing lines of the P-51 Mustang or the majestic grace of the P-38 Lightning. It just looks big, brutal, and mean as a son of a bitch—and it is! But to us, as we sit here two miles up in an ocean of air, looking at the other planes in formation, we see power, dependability, and an airplane worthy of its name. We'd rather be here, right now, than any other place in the world. This is beautiful. We are lucky guys.

Up to now there has been radio silence, but the squadron commander breaks that now. "Bonebreak squadron from Bonebreak leader. Take up battle formation."

We've been flying with about 30 feet between airplanes and 150 feet between flights. Now we'll spread out to three times that distance. It gives less of a target for antiaircraft gunners and allows us more opportunity to see what's going on. As we reach the front, we get the first flak. It's 40-millimeter stuff, but we're at their maximum range, so we don't take evasive action or worry about it. The ground controller who we'll be working with later, after we destroy the guns we're going after, comes on the radio.

"Bonebreak leader, this is Prairie Dog. Do you read, over."

"Roger, Prairie Dog. This is Bonebreak leader. I read you loud and clear, over."

"Bonebreak leader, we have some targets for you. Can you handle it? Over."

"Prairie Dog from Bonebreak leader. We have a primary target but will get back to you later, over."

"Roger, Bonebreak leader. Contact me as soon as you can. This is Prairie Dog, out." Well, we say to ourselfs, they must need some help.

We're now approaching the target. The squadron commander has spotted it and begins to circle, and up comes the flak. This is heavy stuff—88 millimeter. The first is low by about 1,000 feet; everyone holds their altitude and continues to circle, but our flight slides to the outside of the circle and closes up. Our job is to watch for enemy fighters. We hope to hell they show up, but based on past experience, doubt that they will.

Red flight, the first flight led by the squadron commander, has picked out its targets. "Tally ho, Red flight," and we see four planes peel off, one after the other, and head down for the target. It's hard not to watch, but we keep our eyes in the sky and our head turning. The squadron is now very vulnerable to a jump by enemy fighters.

Whap! Whap! Whap! Our plane is thrown over on its side, but we gain control immediately. The flight leader breaks to the right; we follow, and to our left, where we just were, are big, black, ugly bursts. We can see the red centers; that's close. He breaks left again, and the flak is now behind us but getting closer. We've got no choice; we have to stay above the target; we'll have to put up with the flak.

Yellow flight is going down now, but only the flight leader and his wing man. The element leader and his wing man are waiting to see the results of the bombing. The squadron leader is circling at 5,000 feet and looking over the results of the attack. He calls the last half of Yellow flight.

"Yellow three, this is Bonebreak leader. There are two guns only partially destroyed. They are the ones closest to the road. Do you see them?"

"Roger, Bonebreak leader. I see 'em. You want 'em out?"

"Roger, Yellow three. Come down and get 'em."

"Yellow four from Yellow three. Do you see the guns?"

"Roger, Yellow three."

"Yellow four from Yellow three. You take the one nearest the road. I'll take the other one."

"Yellow three from Yellow four, roger. Let's go." The last of Yellow flight starts down, and we're still dodging flak. Our flight leader decides to drop down to 8,000 feet. This flak is just too much, and the last several bursts have been at our exact altitude. If we stay here much longer, we're liable to get blown away.

"Blue leader, this is Bonebreak. I've located some 88s a mile south of the target. Get a sight on 'em, and take 'em out."

"Bonebreak leader, this is Blue leader—roger. We're get'n a hell of a lot of flak up here. I'll try to find 'em."

So those are the bastards. We go to full throttle; everyone is looking, and then we spot one at the edge of the trees lining the road.

"Blue leader from Blue three. I see one at the edge of the trees. It's a mile or so south of the target right next to the road, same side as the target."

"Roger, Blue three. Can you find one for Blue four?"

"Blue two, I've got ours in sight. Follow me in. Take the one to the right." Our flight leader rolls over and heads down for his target with his wing man in formation, but he'll break formation half way down and go for his own gun.

We're looking and straining to see, kicking our airplane every which way to get a better view, and now the flak is beginning to close in on us. Finally, at the side of a farm building on the other side of the road, we spot the other one.

"Blue four from Blue three. Look across the road and just south of that farm building. Do you see it?"

"Roger, Blue three. I see it."

"That's your target, Blue four."

"Roger."

"Blue leader from Blue three. We have our targets. I want to go in."

"Roger, Blue three. They're yours."

By now those flak gunners know what's about to happen. They're going to be attacked by the dreaded Thunderbolt, and they're shooting everything they have, hoping to get us first.

In looking for our target we've gradually lost altitude but picked up speed. We're at 7,000 feet now. We roll over and start down; we can clearly see the gun and crew and a burst from the muzzle sending a high explosive shell our way. The flak is bursting all around us now. We're slipping and skidding the plane, doing half rolls, pointing away from the gun, everything we can do to throw them off. At 3,000 feet we bank the plane, bring the gun sight right on the gun pit, and squeeze the trigger. Our eight 50s begin firing, and even in a dive we can feel their recoil. A hundred rounds a second are pouring into that gun pit. Time is suspended. We don't think or breathe even though we're moving through space at over 400 miles an hour. We're almost ready to drop the bombs—just a split second more; we're under 1,000 feet, right down their throat. Now! We release the bombs and pull up over them clearing the gun by 50 feet. We can hear and feel our bomb explode as we bank left and look back. Wow! A direct hit. We got those kraut bastards.

As we pull up, we begin to feel the G forces pushing us into the seat. But we're only getting about three Gs; that's not enough to black us out, but we're definitely plastered to the seat and have an unnatural and uncomfortable feeling all over our body, but it soon passes.

We roll to the right and check the gun our wing man went after. He got a good hit, and the gun is ruined. Dust and smoke are beginning to settle over both targets.

Suddenly we're aware that we're sweating, breathing hard, and can feel our heart beating in our ears; it's fast and strong. We'd give a lot for a cigarette and an ice-cold coke right now.

# CHAPTER 14: COME FLY WITH ME

Our wing man pulls into formation, and we begin to look for our flight leader.

"Bonebreak squadron, this is Bonebreak leader. Assemble at Angels 10 over the target."

We hear the squadron leaders call and finish the climb to 10,000 feet. We link up with our flight leader. The squadron leader circles low over the target area and satisfies himself that the heavy artillery guns, our primary target, are totally destroyed and then climbs to join the squadron. In addition to those guns there are four 88 antiaircraft guns that will never fire again and a lot of dead Germans.

Once assembled we head for the front lines. All bombs have been expended, but everyone has plenty of 50-caliber machine gun ammunition left. As we reach the front, we hear on the radio, "Prairie Dog, this is Bonebreak leader. Do you read?"

"Roger, Bonebreak leader. This is Prairie Dog; glad you're here. I have targets for you. Please stand by."

"Roger, Prairie Dog. Standing by."

So far everything is going great. The squadron has successfully destroyed the primary target, and we got direct hits on those 88s. We're all circling now, waiting for the ground controller to assign a target.

We don't expect any German fighters, but our eyes are constantly scanning the sky; there is no flak.

"Bonebreak leader, this is Prairie Dog. Proceed to sector A-4. There are some Tiger tanks giving us a problem."

"Roger, Prairie Dog. We're on our way."

Our special grid map will give us the location, but that's not our problem. The squadron leader will get us there. Someone calls out flak at three o'clock just as we look in that direction. It's 40-millimeter stuff and no threat. The squadron holds its course.

We look over the battlefield. There are fires here and there but no big battles going on. Then we spot the tanks—four of them. They are on a hard surfaced road with a line of trees to their north and open fields to their south. We don't call their position; if the squadron leader hasn't seen them, he will shortly, and we'll be considered an impolite jerk if we beat him to it. Even though we're excited, we must stay calm until he's ready. He makes a wide turn to the right starting to circle them.

"Bonebreak squadron, this is Bonebreak leader. We will attack from the side— line abreast—flight by flight. Let's go!"

He rolls over and starts down just as the tanks stop and swing their turrets toward the attack. All the planes in his flight roll over together and get themselves abreast during the dive. You see the muzzle bursts from the tanks as they elevate those deadly 88s. Here comes the flak—big, ugly, black bursts with fiery red centers. It's close, and our plane is knocked around. Yellow flight rolls over but comes in from another heading. Now the tank gunners have to decide who to shoot at. There are two flights coming at them now from different directions. Suddenly there is quad-mount, 20-millimeter fire from the other side of the trees. Now our flight rolls over; we're diving at over 400 miles per hour. We stay in the dive and pull out at 50 feet about a half mile from the tanks. We're coming in broadside, all guns blazing. One tank is burning; suddenly another bursts into flames. Their extra fuel cans have been hit. The fuel pours down into the engine compartment, hits the hot exhaust, and explodes. We pull over him just as the Germans inside open the hatch to escape. Red flight is right behind us firing at the hatch; they can't get out; they're frying. That quadmount 20 is still firing. Yellow leader says he's spotted him and takes his flight in to attack. Our flight leader pulls up to 1,500 feet, rolls over in a tight turn, and dives again at the tanks. It's up to us to stay in formation and be line abreast when we begin firing at the remaining tanks. We feel the G forces, but they're not extreme. Disregard them; we've got work to do. Three of them are now burning, but the front tank is still firing and appears okay. The squadron leader comes on the radio.

"Red flight in trail. We're taking that first tank."

Now he pulls something we've been told will work. When a tank is on a hard surfaced road, you can knock it out by flying directly at it, head on, and shooting a flat trajectory onto the roadway ahead of the tank. The bullets hit the road and ricochet up through the bottom of the tank: the bottom is the least armored and the most vulnerable spot. Once a bullet penetrates the floor and gets inside, it tears the hell out of everything and everybody in there as it flies around like a buzz saw.

He makes the attack and pulls up. Our flight leader comes on the air, "Blue flight, get in trail. We're going for the tracks." We dive down from 1,000 feet, level out on the deck, and come in broadside, aiming for the front sprocket gear that controls the track; shoot that gear out and that tank can't go anywhere. As we come in from the side, the gun turret doesn't turn. The squadron leader's frontal attack may have worked.

We assemble at 2,000 feet and circle the tanks. No one got out of the three tanks that are burning; we're sure of that. The fate of the front tank is in doubt. The crew could be dead or faking it, no longer shooting to make us believe they're dead. There's no way we can tell for sure, but the tank is no longer able to move, so it's effectively out of action.

"Prairie Dog, this is Bonebreak leader. Do you read? Over."

"Roger, Bonebreak. Over."

"Prairie Dog from Bonebreak leader. We have a few minutes left. Do you have a target?"

"Roger, Bonebreak leader. Stand by."

By now we're hot, tired, sweating like a pig, Our throat is dry as a bone. We have a headache and our face hurts—but we feel great. So far it's been a good mission.

"Bonebreak leader, this is Prairie Dog. Head for section B-2 and stand by."

"Roger, Prairie Dog."

We're just a few minutes from the next target as the squadron swings lazily to the new heading.

"Bonebreak leader, start a turn to the right and watch for smoke—now; it is blue."

"Roger, Prairie Dog. I see it."

The color of the smoke is announced just as the smoke shell bursts; this prevents the Germans, who are listening in, from putting smoke on our own troops.

"Bonebreak leader, this is Prairie Dog. There are German troops in the woods just south of the smoke. Let 'em have it."

"Roger, Prairie Dog."

He begins to circle the woods, and now they open up with their quadmount 20s and everything else they've got including their rifles and machine guns.

"Bonebreak squadron, close it up. We're going in by twos."

We pour on power to close up our position. We want to be close enough to the planes ahead of us that we begin to shoot as they're pulling off the target, but be careful, we don't want to hit someone in our own squadron.

The tracers are coming our way in a steady stream. We slip sideways and begin firing. There are German soldiers down there. We can see them, some running, some shooting at us. Our machine guns are screaming. We can smell the cordite, the gasoline fumes, and our own sweat. We shoot for five seconds and pull up in a tight turn to the left and get in position for our next pass. We feel the G forces. We see the tracers from that quadmount 20, but the gun is hidden in the trees. The tracer pattern shifts. He's no longer firing at us but someone pulling off the target. Suddenly we spot him and react instantly.

"Blue leader from Blue three—I'm going for that quadmount. Blue four, take him from the right."

We don't wait for an okay or an acknowledgment. There isn't time. Our wing man is experienced; he knows what to do. He banks to the right to get some distance between us and then turns toward the gun. Now we're both firing at that son of a bitch. The loaders are blown to pieces, and the gunner tries to run for it. He gets about 10 feet, and we see him thrown through the air as he's hit with the full force of our machine guns. We pull up and call our wing man.

"Blue four, we'll take another pass at that gun—in trail."

"Roger, Blue three."

He drops behind us as we start our strafing run, but this time from the back side of the gun. We shoot a 4-second burst, and during that time our guns have hit the apex, and all bullets are hitting within a very small circle; gun parts begin flying off. We pull up, and our wing man finishes it off.

As we fired that last burst, we notice a stream of tracers coming from our own guns; that signals we're nearing the last of our ammunition; it's time to go home. Thankfully, we hear over the radio:

"Bonebreak squadron from Bonebreak leader. Assemble at Angels 5. We're going home. Prairie Dog from Bonebreak leader. We've got to leave you, but those woods are clear."

"Roger, Bonebreak leader. Thanks a lot. We can get moving down here now, over and out."

"Thanks for the targets, Prairie Dog. This is Bonebreak leader. Good luck—roger and out."

We assemble at 5,000 feet over the woods we've just strafed. No one is firing at us now. We're sweating like a pig, throat sore, arms sore; the oxygen mask is breaking the bridge of our nose; our ears hurt from the headphones, and the air we're breathing smells like a garbage pit; we'd give a million dollars for a cigarette. We're in close formation now and thoroughly wrung out, but our squadron has done its job; we've killed Germans and saved American G.I.s; that's what we're here for. As we near the field, we hear over the radio:

"Bonebreak leader to Bonebreak squadron. Does anyone have any battle damage?" No one answers. If they did, they'd be the last to land because a damaged plane could crash on landing and put the runway out of service. With everyone very low on fuel, that could spell disaster.

It's our flight's turn to land. We come low and fast over the end of the field in perfect tight formation, and all break up into a semi-loop, each plane widening the turn to give a 15-second separation between landings.

As we pull up into that semi-loop, we start our landing procedure; we lock our shoulder straps, at the top of the loop drop our wheels and flaps, and open and lock the canopy; our face hurts; we wonder why someone can't design a more comfortable oxygen mask.

Ease it down. Don't bounce. Put on a show for the ground crews. Hold it off. Let it settle and thump! We're on the ground and rolling smoothly down the runway.

The crew chief is waiting as we turn off the runway. We stop just long enough for him to jump up on the wing, and he guides us to our parking area. When we're parked, we lock the brakes and turn the switch off. The prop slowly grinds to a stop. The mission is over.

The crew chief is sticking his face in the cockpit, unstrapping our belt and smiling from ear to ear. We unhook that torturous oxygen mask, take our helmet off, and rub our face.

The letdown now hits like a ton of bricks. It takes all our remaining strength to get out of the cockpit and down to the ground; he brings our chute. A jeep pulls up. A guy runs to our plane and retrieves the gun camera film, replaces a new magazine, and heads for the next plane.

Now we reach for that cigarette, offer the crew chief one, and he pulls out his Zippo, lighting us up. His assistant comes over and tells us we have four holes in the belly and three in the tail. That's no surprise; there was a lot of flak. We tell them what the target was—what we personally hit—how the battle went. They're eager for the details. We tell them we got one Tiger tank, one 88 flak gun, a quadmount 20, and a hell of a lot of Germans. The other pilots are telling their stories to their crews. There were only six big guns, four 88 antiaircraft guns, four Tiger tanks, and two quadmount 20s, plus a hell of a lot of Germans destroyed. But that night in their tents, they'll brag about what their pilot did. If they have to, they'll expand it a bit, maybe quite a bit. They'll brag about the holes in their airplane; that proves their pilot was right in the thick of the heaviest fighting. By morning, if you'd add up the total of what each crew chief claims his pilot destroyed, it would easily be double or triple the actual score. But they are proud of their pilots, and by God, no other crew chief is going to top them.

The jeep comes by and takes us to the equipment tent. We put our chutes on the table—they will be closely examined before being replaced on the shelf—hang up our helmet with its built-in torture devices for your ears, nose, and chin, and retrieve our hat. The waiting jeep takes us to critique (it's now called debriefing).

The intelligence officer is waiting to hear the story of the mission. The report is given by rank and seniority, first the squadron leader, then the flight leaders, and finally, the rest of us. We state our claims and report on the flak. The clerk collects our escape kit and returns our personal stuff.

After critique is completed, we head for our tent. There's sort of a depression now, a letdown; we're sore; we're tired, actually, exhausted. The adrenaline is long gone, but it was a good mission, a good fight. We made it back, one more mission to our credit. We realize there were hundreds of Thunderbolts out today on similar missions—some didn't come back—but the Germans paid a terrible price in today's fighting, and we had the chance to experience and share the glory.

Suddenly we realize that we stink; time to head for the shower and get cleaned up. It's nearly time for dinner. Tonight after dinner we'll go over the details of the mission with our friends. We'll all exchange ideas. Did we attack the target correctly? Did anyone notice a change in tactics of the antiaircraft gunners. We talk about the squadron commanders head-on attack on that tank. Did his bullets actually ricochet up through the bottom of the tank? There's a new replacement pilot, who has just joined the squadron, listening to the conversation. We explain to him how two planes can attack a quadmount 20 at the same time. He listens. He's eager, and we hope he lasts awhile.

We're not on the morning mission, so we can get as drunk as we want. Pour another drink. Christ! If they ever run out of this stuff, we'll lose the war.

## chapter 15

# POW

There were thousands of American airmen shot down during World War II, and the Germans made special provisions for them. Interrogating downed pilots was a way to get information on the makeup and strength of individual squadrons and groups. Fighter and fighter-bomber pilots were interrogated by a separate section of German Intelligence.

In my squadron, our casualty rate was about average when compared to other squadrons doing the same work, and of all our pilots shot down over enemy territory, only two became prisoners of war—all the rest were killed.

In the Eighth Air Force the majority of pilots shot down ended up POWs and lived to survive the war. Why the big difference? The answer lies in the combat role of the fighter-bomber pilot. It was his job to attack ground targets, most of which were heavily defended. During the big battles of the ground war in Europe, he was right in the thick of it, flying on the deck—shooting it out with tanks, antiaircraft guns, and every kind of armored vehicle the Germans had. He strafed troop columns, went after machine gun nests, fortified positions, and anywhere he could find German soldiers.

Follow this typical scenario: There is a full-scale battle going on involving tens of thousands of troops. The Americans are pushing the Germans back, but the Germans are resisting furiously. The fighter-bombers are at work; their mission is to spend one hour over the target area and attack any targets assigned to them by their ground controller. Let's assume the assigned target is a column of German Tiger tanks in support of German infantry; in addition there are some other armored vehicles with them.

The controller gives the location of the Germans, and the fighter-bombers proceed to that sector and spot them; all flights attack. The P-47s' eight 50-caliber machine guns are more than enough to knock out a tank, especially at this point in the war. The German tanks were short of fuel, and their supply lines were so disrupted that refueling was a major problem. To counter this situation, they would carry extra fuel in "Jerry cans" lashed on the back of the tank behind the turret; this placed those cans above the engine. The fighter-bombers would fly over the column of tanks shooting at the gas cans.

## CHAPTER 15: POW

The cans were shot to pieces; the fuel ran down into the engine compartment, hit the hot exhaust, and burst into flames. The crew would be closed up inside the tank during the attack, but in order to keep from being cooked, they had to get out; as they opened the main hatch, the next fighter-bomber in line of attack would fly over the column and shoot at the hatch. In desperation, as they were being burned alive, they'd try to get out anyway, regardless of the incoming machine gun fire, but they rarely made it.

Next the fighter-bomber would turn on the remaining armored vehicles and infantry. This battle could last as long as 10 minutes, and during that time many of the Germans would be slaughtered, but they would put up one hell of a fight and shoot everything they had from the individual infantryman's rifle to the Tiger tank's dreaded 88 and everything in between.

In the middle of the battle one of the fighter-bombers is hit. His plane is on fire, but he's too low to bail out. Fortunately he has enough speed to pull up to 3,000 feet, then bails out. He floats down a short distance from the battle but well within reach of the German infantrymen who have just seen the crews of their tanks and armored column cremated and most of their buddies blown apart. Now, do you expect these same soldiers to capture that pilot and say, "Under the Geneva Convention you are a prisoner of war and will be treated as such?" If you do, you don't understand the human psyche. They are caught up in the blood lust of battle. They want revenge and intend to get it. That pilot can only hope for a quick bullet in the head. In most cases the pilot stuck with the plane, attempted to fly it as far away from the battle scene as possible before crashing. But one way or the other, his chances were practically zilch.

In the majority of cases, however, the pilot got hit on his attack run and never had a chance to pull out. When you were working between 20 feet and 1,000 feet and at speeds of 350 to 450 miles per hour, there wasn't much time to do a hell of a lot about it. If you got hit, you bought the farm; it was that simple.

One of our pilots who became a POW defied all odds by going down in the middle of a particularly fierce battle and living to tell about it.

He told the story to me in October of 1989. An experience such as his leaves indelible imprints, and he recalled the details as if the incident had just recently occurred. Here is his story in first person:

I was flying as element leader in a flight of four Thunderbolts on a ground support mission near Eperney, France; it was mid-August 1944. We had been directed by our front line ground controller to an area of German soldiers. We located them and strafed them, then we observed some tanks. We were carrying 500-pound bombs, so we attacked the tanks by dive-bombing and then went back in to strafe the personnel and the other armored support vehicles that were with the tanks. There were many vehicles and just four of us, and I guess I got greedy and on the second pass made the cardinal mistake of attacking the column lengthwise instead of hitting them from the side. We were getting a lot of flak when all at once I took a burst in the engine. At that point I was about 30 feet above the deck. I knew that was it, so I began climbing immediately for enough altitude to bail out, but I had a hell of a time getting out. As I rolled over to drop out, the front of the plane dived down, and I couldn't get out. I got back into the seat, grabbed the controls, did a half roll, and went over the side. By now I was only about 500 feet or so. My chute popped open, but so help me, to this day, I have no recollection of pulling the rip cord; it must have been an automatic reaction. Anyway, I made one swing in the chute and hit the ground.

I got out of my chute, pulled my 45 from the holster, and threw it as far as I could throw it. I figured I'd have a better chance unarmed because I was right in the middle of the battle area, and I sure as hell couldn't take on the whole German army with a pistol. I took off running, spotted a hedgerow, and headed for it. I stuck my head through, and there was a German soldier looking right at me with his rifle pointed straight between my eyes. He took me to a German jeep that was parked nearby and motioned to the passenger seat; I got in. There was an officer driving, and the soldier got in the back seat and put the muzzle of his rifle in the back of my neck. You've heard the term "cold steel." Well believe me, that son of a bitch was cold, and it never warmed up. Suddenly I had an overwhelming desire to sleep, but I was afraid if I nodded off and my head wavered that guy behind me would blow me apart.

They drove me to the headquarters of the unit we had just strafed and brought me to their colonel. He looked me over and told me I was captured, and there was nothing I could do about it. He treated me well, gave me a cup of coffee, and then I was taken to their rear lines, eventually linking up with other prisoners of war. Fortunately I was captured by a German army unit rather than an SS outfit.

I was kept on the move; that night I slept in a chicken house. It was uncomfortable but not as bad as I expected. I was wearing my summer flying suit and flight jacket. During August during the day it was warm, but it got damn cold at night. I traveled for several days with this group of prisoners, and we were under heavy guard at all times. All the while the number of prisoners increased. Finally, there were about 70 of us.

Late one afternoon we were in the back of an open truck, part of a column of about five or six trucks, when I noticed a flight of P-38s heading in the opposite direction. Suddenly the leader did a slight wingover, and I knew what was coming. I yelled, and all the trucks stopped. Everyone jumped out and headed for the ditch; I took the left side; others took the right. My guard was a very young, very short boy, and he stayed with me. I ran out into the field and hit the ground. He seemed a little confused, but he followed my example. I'd run, and as a plane came in on its strafing run, I'd hit the ground and pushed him down with me.

When the P-38s pulled away, we went back to the truck and found that all the Americans who had taken shelter on the right side had been killed; the ones who went left survived. My little guard, although he couldn't speak any English, expressed his gratitude to me with a pat on my shoulder.

We couldn't do anything for the dead guys, so they herded us back into the truck, and we left. I don't know what finally happened to the bodies, but the American army was not far behind, so I suppose the Germans may have left them there because they were Americans and could be properly buried by our own people.

# CHAPTER 15: POW

Our truck was still okay, so we continued east. We were then put on a train, and a couple of days later, while we were in a marshaling yard, B-17s came over and bombed the place. It was a hell of an experience and the third time that fate was on my side. Later, during the train ride, I decided to try to escape. There were about 75 of us in that box car, about half air corps and half ground troops. The army guys stayed by themselves, and so did we. I don't know why, but we had voluntarily segregated ourselves. Anyway, the air corps guys were all for trying it, and I was able to get the door unlocked. We got the door open just as the train began to slow and prepared to start jumping out. The ground guys must have seen some pretty rough combat because they told us not to try it, and if we did, they'd yell for the guards. I can't explain the difference in attitude between ourselves and the ground guys. I do know that we had extensive training in escape and evasion tactics, were all officers, and were conditioned to make every effort to escape, but in any event, we had to forget our escape attempt. Again, this may have been the fourth time fate intervened on my behalf. Had we tried and failed I would have been dead.

We eventually arrived at Metz, and at that point we were separated. Three of us were sent to Oberrusso, which was a town near Frankfurt, Germany. I later learned that all fighter and fighter-bomber pilots were sent to this place first.

While we were waiting for our train in Frankfurt, our guards walked away and left us. However, there were lots of civilians watching us. Besides myself there was another Thunderbolt pilot and a pilot with the Free French forces. He was in full dress uniform and soon began hurling insults at the German civilians, and we couldn't shut the bastard up. They moved in toward us, and then came a group with three ropes: I could see us all dangling from some nearby girders. I was really scared, so scared I didn't know what to do. Anyway, they closed to within a few feet of us with the ropes at the ready, and I figured this was it. At that point our guards came back and shooed them away. Again my ass had been saved.

At Oberrusso I was immediately put into solitary confinement; that's an experience that just can't be described. I was kept there for two weeks. No one talked to me, and I didn't know what to expect. There was an opaque window in my cell, and I finally was able to pry it open with some nails I got out of my bunk. They fed me; it wasn't good, but it was probably not a hell of a lot worse than what the guards were eating. The room was very small, painted white, with a straw mattress on a wooden bunk. When I had to go to the can, I pulled a lever which raised a flag outside of the cell. A guard would come and escort me to the can and back to my cell. No matter what I said or asked him, he would not speak to me. That silent treatment continued all the time I was in solitary.

Finally my wait was over, and they took me to interrogation. I was addressed by my name and rank, offered a seat, and given a cup of real coffee and a cigarette. The interrogation was nothing like I expected. There was a large map on the wall, and he asked me where my squadron was located, and I told him I wouldn't tell him. He asked where we would move to next; I didn't know, but I gave him the same answer. He opened a file on his desk and started reading. He told me my squadron and group number and the name of the commanding officer. He told me names of other pilots in the squadron, and then I noticed there was a prominent pin on a large wall map behind his desk at my group's location with the group and squadron numbers attached. He really didn't seem interested in whether I gave him any answers or not.

I was trained to give my name, rank, and serial number only. Anything else, I was told, would give aid and comfort to the enemy. This turned out to be ridiculous because he knew everything about me and my unit, had a complete dossier on me, and shocked me by telling me my mother's maiden name and where I'd graduated from. I later found out the Germans had a clipping service in America that forwarded all information on pilots that they picked up from newspapers and other contacts.

After this reasonably pleasant interrogation I was sent on to prison camp. Air corps personnel were sent to special camps called stalags, and I ended up at Barth, Germany.

What followed was nine months of boredom, hunger, cold, and anxiety. For me the war was over, but I would have to endure this as best I could until the Germans were defeated. I was issued a blanket and a knit hat, and when my flying suit wore out, they gave me some pants. I was never mistreated, but the food was horrible, and we understood our guards weren't eating much better. Cigarettes were scarce and only available in the Red Cross packages, which we received occasionally. We had a dispensary with American medical people, but fortunately I never had to use it.

In the group of pilots I was with there were just two P-47 Thunderbolt fighter-bomber pilots; the rest were bomber and fighter pilots from the Eighth Air Force.

In reflecting on this experience, I considered myself very lucky. I could have been shot when I was first captured. After all, I had just killed a lot of their comrades. I could have been killed when we were strafed by the P-38s. They naturally assumed we were Germans and a legitimate target, or American bombs from the B-17s could have finished me. If I continued with my escape attempt, I could have been killed or later could have been hanged by German civilians who were surely bent on killing us—but our guards intervened. There is no way to account for my survival. I defied all odds. The fortunes of war were on my side.

Author's note: After his ordeal of World War II, he answered the call again as a reserve officer, flying a full tour of combat duty in the Korean War.

# chapter 16

# RETRIBUTION

One day we were getting some sack time on a hot August afternoon. There were no missions on tap, and not even a schedule had been posted. There was apparently a temporary lull in the fighting, and we were taking advantage of it.

Without any preamble, the squadron clerk came running from tent to tent calling all pilots to a hurry-up meeting. We went to the briefing tent, and when we were all gathered, the squadron commander told us we were going on an immediate mission and then turned the briefing over to the intelligence office.

He placed his pointer on the map at a location a few miles to the rear of the front lines.

"Gentlemen, we just received a report that a German unit pulled out of this place a few hours ago." He paused for effect and then continued, "But before they left they lined up all the males in the village, kids included, and executed them—just shot them in cold blood. We've been ordered to find this unit and completely annihilate them."

This was a real shock, and we were all stunned.

"You mean they killed them for no reason?" someone asked.

"The only reason we know about was they were French, and those SS bastards are ruthless mother-fuckers."

"Jesus Christ, let's get those bastards!"

Briefing was short. There were two roads leading from this town; one heading northeast and the other southeast; the Germans were retreating using both roads. Our mission was to find, attack, and destroy those troops on the southeast road. Another squadron was assigned to the northeast road.

While we were being briefed, our planes were being armed with some high explosive but mostly clusters of fragmentation antipersonnel bombs. This type of bomb was designed to be used against ground troops. When it exploded, it produced the maximum amount of shrapnel.

We flew over the village, picked up the southeast road, and followed it out until we spotted them. As soon as we started to circle, the half tracks and other light armored vehicles left the road and scattered to the open farmland on either side. The trucks stopped, and the troops jumped out to take cover; the tanks stayed on the road.

"Bonebreak squadron, this is Bonebreak leader. Red flight will take the tanks. Yellow flight take the half tracks on the south side, right-hand pattern; Blue flight the north side, left-hand pattern. Use your discretion on expending bombs. Let's go. Red flight, arm your bombs."

By now we were getting lots of flak. The tanks had the big 88 millimeters, and the half tracks had the 20s. Because three separate flights would be attacking separate targets, we had to be especially careful to avoid a midair collision.

"Yellow flight, this is Yellow leader. Stay low; we don't want to tangle with Red flight. Acknowledge."

"Yellow two, Roger."

"Yellow three, Roger."

"Yellow four, Roger."

"Blue flight from Blue leader. You heard Yellow leader; we're doing the same; left-hand pattern, only stay low. Acknowledge."

"Blue two, Roger."

"Blue three, Roger."

"Blue four, Roger."

And so the battle started. It was fierce but short-lived. Within five minutes the armor was on fire, and most of their crews dead. After that we made pass after pass strafing the column and sides of the road. There's no question some of those soldiers survived, but the vast majority did not. What we left was utter destruction. Our high command wanted to deliver a message: whatever troops were involved in such an atrocity would be hunted down and slaughtered.

There was only one weapon that could be used for such retribution, and that was the P-47 Thunderbolt. So in addition to being a front line combat weapons system, it took on a quasi-political role, and apparently the lesson was not lost on the German high command.

We realized now that their high command was fragmented. There was the German army and the Nazi SS. The German army still respected the rules of warfare, the obligation of victor to the vanquished, and the basic rights of humans. The Nazi SS paid no attention to this code of honor. They were sadistic butchers.

We knew nothing of the source of details of the male slaughter in the village. We only knew what we were told and what our mission assignment was. It was just another day in the blood-and-guts drive across Europe against the Germans.

We had not seen the last of atrocities. In December in a town called Malmedy, the Germans assembled a number of American prisoners (about 300). They took them out of town and lined them up in an open field; there was snow on the ground. Suddenly the canvas coverings on the trucks that surrounded our soldiers were dropped, and the hidden machine guns opened up. They didn't stop until all of these defenseless American prisoners were killed—or so they thought. When the shooting started, some prisoners automatically hit the deck. Because the soldiers were standing close together, some fell on top of them. After the automatic fire stopped, individual Germans walked through the group of prisoners and shot any who were still alive. But with bodies piled on top of bodies, some were still alive, and they stayed motionless, playing dead for hours until they felt it was safe to escape. One or two, in the immediate confusion at the start of the executions, ran to the nearby forest and hid. Within a short time these survivors made it back to American lines and told the story of this murderous act.

The news spread to the American forces quickly; another hurry-up call for a pilots' meeting, and when we assembled in the briefing room, we were given the story that I have just related. The war had taken a terrible turn. There was no longer any form of honor on the battlefield. From here on it would be a no-holds-barred fight. There were rumors that Hitler had issued orders that P-47 fighter-bomber pilots were not to be treated as prisoners of war but as criminals and were to be summarily executed. We were called Roosevelt's Gangsters, and they called the P-47 Jabo, which translates to something like lightning from the sky. We were told, from then on, that if we were hit, to make every attempt to get to a Luftwaffe base before bailing out. There we would be treated like fellow airmen, even though we were on opposite sides.

This new and disturbing information had a telling effect on the pilots. We realized our chances were close to nothing of surviving if we got shot down, but to find out that the Germans had no qualms about executing helpless prisoners was a real shock. The chance of finding a German Luftwaffe base was slim to none because we were mostly working near the front lines, and the Luftwaffe bases were well to the rear. The decision, if it had to be made, would be a split second one. You could go in with your plane, all guns blazing, taking as many Germans with you as you could, and die in a spasm of glory, fighting till the end, or take a chance on survival but most likely die like a trussed-up animal being slaughtered. What decision would you make?

The killing of defenseless American prisoners of war was well documented. There was another documented case that occurred earlier in the campaign involving French civilians in the town of Oradour-sur-Glâne. The SS shot all the men then burned the women and children to death. Premeditated acts of wanton killing of defenseless soldiers and civilians are absolutely unforgivable. Atrocities committed during the blood lust of battle, committed instantly as a reaction to a preceding event, may be excusable under certain circumstances; the point is, these things do happen. But were the atrocities all on the other side? War and atrocities go together, just as war and death are inseparably linked.

The Thunderbolt fighter-bomber was the greatest killing machine in close-in fighting that the American forces had. The Germans, having nothing comparable of their own, considered it an unfair weapon. I talked to a pilot who had been shot down and captured and because of the great disarray at the time was taken to the rear of the German lines and passed off from one unit to another until he was finally placed with a group of other captured airmen, the remnants of two B-17 bomber crews. None of them had so far been interrogated. Finally a German SS officer took charge of them and, with a few enlisted men, began transporting them to a POW camp. They were being treated well and fed the same rations as their guards. One of the airmen, a waist gunner, spoke a little German and constantly thanked the SS officer for his humane treatment. The SS officer said he had no animosity toward the bomber pilots, but if he caught a Jabo pilot, he would personally slit his throat, and he meant it. Jabo was what the Germans called the Thunderbolt. My friend then identified himself as a B-24 bomber pilot. Of course, the other airmen knew he was a Thunderbolt pilot, but the German SS officer never learned the truth.

To close this little incident, I'll tell you the rest of the story, and it has a happy ending. As they continued moving, sometimes hitching rides on trucks and trains and sometimes walking, the war was catching up with them. Finally they were hearing the heavy guns of the advancing American troops. Under the circumstances the German SS officer lost interest in them, put a corporal in charge, and took off to join the retreat. The waist gunner talked the German corporal into giving up, and the whole bunch of them hid in a town until the Americans overran their position and they were safe. They made sure the corporal and his men had plenty of cigarettes, gum, chocolate, and a couple of K-rations and bid them farewell. The Germans were quite happy to be POWs.

My friend's entire capture and escape took 12 days, and two weeks from the day he was shot down he was back with the squadron. His tale of the SS officer's hate of the Thunderbolt pilots was just another piece of bad news for us, but we were getting the same information in our briefings from our own intelligence people, so even though it was bad news, it was not new news.

But what about us? What about our side? I've talked with infantry soldiers who said they personally knew of cases where our guys shot captured German prisoners when they were supposed to be taking them to a rear position for interrogation and entry into the POW process. The simple alibi was that the prisoners tried to escape, so they shot them. Anyone who believes this never happened is naive and does not understand life under combat conditions.

As the war progressed, things got nastier, especially after we started using napalm bombs, which was about September 1944. We had scrupulously avoided ever shooting at a vehicle displaying a red cross. But as things got tougher for the Germans, they began placing ambulances in their regular truck or armored columns. Naturally we hit those columns and made every effort to miss the ambulances but were not always successful in that endeavor. To our surprise those ambulances, supposedly carrying wounded soldiers, blew up with the same intensity as an ammunition truck. The Germans had used the red cross as a guise to transport ammunition in ambulances. So the escalation of dishonor continued. From then on we paid no attention to the red cross and attacked whenever and wherever we found them.

Food was a necessity, so food supplies were legitimate targets. But what about a cow browsing in a pasture? Was it a legitimate target? Whether it was or not we killed them whenever we spotted them. It was becoming an all-out war—no holds barred—nothing sacred—nothing spared.

By November we began getting reports of Thunderbolt pilots being killed by German civilians. In retaliation, civilians became fair game. We bombed and strafed railroad depots and villages, even though there was no military presence observable. Of course these were not primary targets, but if we had not found military targets by the time we had to leave our assigned target area, rather than jettison the bombs in an open field, we used them on civilians.

After the war I learned that one of my friends had met his death at the hands of German civilians. He had been hit at the target but was able to keep the plane flying for 10 minutes or so; that put him well away from the target and over open farm country. At that point he lost power and had to bail out. We knew his location and reported to our intelligence people where he went down.

Investigation after the war uncovered the rest of the story. He was captured by the local townspeople—no military involved. They beat him up, pushed him against a wall, and killed him by repeatedly jabbing him with pitch forks. That's a hell of a way for a fighting man to die—especially a fighter-bomber pilot.

War brings out the absolute worst in the men who do the fighting. They are the ones who experience the horror, see the death, and in self-defense, for their own survival, make themselves immune to it. In the blood lust of combat any despicable action is possible and justifiable at the time. Only later, in the calm of public reflection and courtroom proceedings can the picture be brought into focus and judgment rendered—but those who judge are not the ones who have experienced the hell of the soul, the torment of the mind, and the ever-present mental photograph of the instant, permanently burned into the brain. Perhaps only God can decide, but where the hell was He when we needed Him?

chapter 17

# THE PERFECT MISSION

Awell-executed mission was like a symphony; everyone did exactly what they were supposed to do at the precise time, and the outcome was a dramatic success—but things didn't always work that way. In fact, the perfect mission was actually the exception. Let's ride along on what started out as a well-planned mission that should have been near perfect and see what actually happened.

The mission was called for 1000 hours, which meant we could get up at the regular time, have a leisurely breakfast, with plenty of time to go to the can and psyche ourselves up for the coming event.

The target was a concentration of heavy gun emplacements that had been shelling our troops and exacting heavy casualties for days. The guns had been located, and aerial reconnaissance had photographed them. They were about 10 miles into German territory and right at the intersection of two major roads. There was a canal a few hundred yards east of their position that would aid in locating them. They were defended by six quadmount 20-millimeter rapid fire antiaircraft guns; there were probably more hidden in some nearby trees.

Briefing was called for 0900 hours. The operations officer described the target and showed us the pictures; there were four heavy guns. The weather officer told us we could expect overcast from 18,000 feet to about 25,000 feet, but from 18,000 to the ground it would be clear. The intelligence officer pointed out what flak we could expect, and we were routed around any known flak batteries. The quadmount 20s, however, would be vicious at the target.

The squadron commander gave us the plan of attack. Because of the heavy casualties our ground troops were taking, it was absolutely vital to destroy those guns. He would lead the attack, and each plane in his flight would go for a separate gun. Each pilot was given a specific gun based on the aerial photographs. The rest of the squadron would hold their position until the first flight had bombed—then, if any guns remained intact, the flight leader of the second flight would determine how he would attack. The last flight would continue to hold their position until the results of that attack were known, and then, if any guns still remained, it would be up to the last flight leader to see that they were destroyed.

**104**

# CHAPTER 17: THE PERFECT MISSION

Because of our extreme accuracy, it was anticipated that the first flight would destroy the four guns and crew, so alternate targets would be sought for the remaining planes. The weather at our base was 100 percent overcast at 8,000 feet. We would climb through this until we broke into the clear and proceed to the target. Because of the 25,000-foot cloud deck, we would have a long climb on instruments. This was the only worrisome part of the operation; weather could raise hell with the best-planned mission.

Our alternative was to go in under the clouds, but if we did that, we'd draw a lot more flak. In any event, the squadron commander would make the decision after we got under way. We expected heavy flak from the quadmount 20s during the attack; however, we were only 10 miles into enemy territory, less than two minutes flying time. If anyone got hit, he would immediately head for our own lines and hopefully make it there before crashing or bailing out.

This looked to be an ideal mission. The operations officer, due to the importance of the target, had selected the hottest pilots in the squadron to fly this one, and our squadron commander would lead. The squadron commander did not lead every mission. Some time it would be the operations officer or a senior flight leader who led the squadron, but whoever it was, regardless of rank, was called the squadron leader for that mission.

Just as we were heading for the airplanes, the mission was put on hold. For some reason someone in higher command wanted a delay, so we returned to the ready-room and waited.

Finally, at 1400 hours the mission was called, but unfortunately the squadron commander had other duties and had to assign a senior flight leader to take his place. Although he was a fairly good flight leader, he made a lousy squadron leader but, in any event, we were stuck with him.

We got off the ground in record time—20 seconds between airplanes—assembled, and began the long climb to the target. I was flying as element leader of the last flight. My flight leader was flying his brand new D-28 bubble canopy P-47. It was on its maiden voyage. About two minutes into the climb his engine seized and stopped dead, and he began to drop like a rock. There was open pasture land behind him, and he made the turn, heading in for a belly landing. I followed him down waiting for him to jettison his bombs. Finally at 1,000 feet I called him, "Blue leader, get rid of your bombs," and he promptly did. He made a perfect belly landing, slid to a stop, got out of the plane, and waved. I wagged my wings in answer and headed up to rejoin the squadron. The squadron commander radioed his position, and he was home waiting for us when we returned. That night we were drinking together, and he thanked me for reminding him to dump his bombs. He said he was so ticked off at having to damage his new airplane that he completely forgot about them.

So far our perfect mission had three screw-ups, and we were just getting underway. But that was nothing to what was in store for us.

The weather had changed in our favor. We hit the overcast at 10,000 and were on top, in the clear, at 15,000. We stayed at that altitude, continuing toward the target. The weather was breaking up, and when we reached the target area, there was only a 50-percent cloud cover at 12,000 feet. The squadron leader had trouble finding the target but finally decided he had located it. I was leading the last flight—due to my flight leader's earlier mishap—and I couldn't see any gun emplacements, nor was there a canal where it should have been.

"This is Bonebreak leader. I have the target in sight."

"Bonebreak leader, this is Yellow leader. I don't see the target."

"Bonebreak leader, this is Blue leader. I don't see the canal. Isn't it our check point?"

We had now started to circle a road intersection, and at this point all hell seemed to break loose. We were getting intense flak, and from the initial salvo, it looked like we were in for it.

"This is Bonebreak leader to Bonebreak squadron. The guns are in the trees southeast of the road intersection. Arm your bombs."

There was an immediate response.

"Bonebreak leader, this is Yellow leader. I still don't see the target. I think we're south of it."

After a very short pause the squadron leader came back on the radio.

"Bonebreak squadron from Bonebreak leader. We'll attack now—in trail." And he rolled over and started down. I still wasn't able to see any heavy guns, but when the squadron leader orders an attack—you attack.

There are several ways to attack a target. One is to string the squadron out in a big circle above the target, and as each one gets to a designated point, they peel off and head down the chute. It's called attacking in trail. This means every plane comes in at the same angle and from the same compass point at about 10 second intervals, which gives time for the bombs from the previous plane to explode before the next plane is on the target and releases its bombs. It's a favorite approach on a target that's not heavily defended; it's the worst plan of attack if it is; the squadron leader screwed up again; we attacked in trail.

We were at 12,000 feet and would dive and release our bombs at 300 feet. Our speed at that point would be about 450 miles per hour. The disadvantage to this tactic is that the antiaircraft gunners can rapidly adjust their angle of fire at the planes because every plane is coming in from the same direction, at the same angle of dive, and at the same speed. If you're the last man in, you're in deep trouble. The flak was intensifying, and as it came my turn to roll over and start down, I felt and heard a tremendous explosion under the rear of my plane. The next thing I knew, the tail had been flipped up, and I was going over upside down. It was wintertime, and the mud on the cockpit floor from the previous flight had dried, changed to dirt, and had not been cleaned up. The dirt, obeying the laws of physics, flew up toward the top of the canopy and into my eyes. Like an jerk, I didn't have my goggles on; I was temporarily blinded, upside down, falling out of control from 12,000 feet, and every fucking Heinie for miles around was trying to finish me off. When I got control of the plane, I was heading straight down, and God knows how fast. I started to pull it out of that deadly dive, and as I passed about a 30-degree angle, I saw where all the flak was coming from. Straight in front of me was a small building set off by itself from other factory buildings about half a mile away and surrounded by flak guns. It probably was no more than 100 by 200 feet. They were putting everything up from quadmount 20s to the famed German 88.

I made a split-second decision to go for it, feeling it must be important to be so frantically defended and also to be all by its lonesome out in that field well away from everything else. I took evasive action by twisting and turning and then started to turn left away from the target and at the last second racked the plane into a half roll to the right and settled right in line with the building. I was determined to plaster it after what I'd been through. My eyes were stinging and watering, and I was yelling and cursing as I put two 500-pound bombs right through the roof. I felt the first explosion, but it was nothing. A split second later there was one hell of an explosion and then another and another. I was pulling away fast—probably close to 400 miles an hour—but I barely escaped the pressure waves.

The rest of the squadron had bombed the road intersection and climbed back to assemble at 12,000 feet. Over the radio I heard my element leader say, "Bonebreak leader, this is Blue three. Blue leader was hit, and I saw him going down out of control."

"Blue three from Bonebreak leader. Did you see him hit?"

"Negative, but there are big explosions going on about where he would have hit."

I had been concentrating on getting away from those explosions and getting back up to join the squadron when I realized they were talking about me.

"Bonebreak leader—Bonebreak leader, this is Blue leader. I'll join up in a minute. I have you in sight."

"Bonebreak Blue leader, are you okay?"

"Roger, Bonebreak leader, but I'm sure I have battle damage. Let's get out of here."

When I reached them, the smoke from the factory was, by then, up to 10,000 feet and climbing. At this point we were not getting any flak. I think the initial explosions had knocked out the guns. We circled once and saw other explosions; the building was blowing itself to pieces; the smoke column was higher than we were and still climbing. Whatever was in that building was the most volatile material I'd ever seen. Perhaps it was rocket fuel for their V-2s or something experimental. I was never able to find out, but whatever it was met a fiery death and so did the flak crews that were supposed to defend it.

The second flight was missing one plane. No one saw him get hit or go in, and he didn't even call in distress. He simply wasn't there. We headed home.

In November it gets dark early in Europe. Because the mission was delayed and didn't get off the ground until after 1400 hours, we were now returning at twilight which lasts about five minutes, and then it's dark. Our air force didn't fly at night, so anything in the sky was considered enemy.

The Joint Operations Control Center (J.O.C.) was trying to clear us with our own antiaircraft emplacements but wasn't 100 percent successful; soon we were being shot at. It's bad enough to get shot at by the Germans, after all they had a reason, but it absolutely frosts you to be shot at by your own side. Fortunately none of us got hit, and soon we were making a night landing, without landing lights, at a blacked-out field. That type of landing has an asshole-pucker rating of 11 on a scale of 1 to 10.

So what could have been and should have been a perfect mission turned out to be an absolute fiasco. We lost one pilot and his plane; another plane (my flight leader's) was damaged; my plane had several holes in its end and in one wing; two other planes also had sustained some flak damage. The primary target—the guns we were supposed to hit—were still firing; the squadron leader had missed them by about 30 miles. The only good part was the building I blew up, but that came about by pure chance.

We had an interesting meeting that night while we were getting drunk. There were four of us. Jim started the conversation.

"Heard you had a rough mission."

"Yah, rough and completely fucked up. The worst God damn mission I've ever been on."

"Did you hit the target?"

"Hit it? Shit—we didn't even find it. Asshole Mac was leading. We had aerial photos and two perfect check points, but he decided the guns were in some trees, so he leads the whole God damn squadron down to bomb the fuckin' trees."

"Who was leading Yellow flight?"

"Morgan."

"Morgan's good. What did he say?"

"He told that asshole we were south of the target, but it didn't do any good; he ordered the attack."

"How bad you get hit?"

"I was surprised. Only a few small holes, but it flipped me upside down. God damn, that was a hairy son of a bitch.

'But the worst was, there was dirt on the floor, and when I went ass end over, the dirt flew up and into my eyes. It hurt like a son of a bitch, and I couldn't see anything."

"Where were your goggles?"

"On top of my helmet."

"Jesus Christ, Glenn. You asshole. You know better than that; you damn near killed yourself."

"I know it, but I'm hauling that crew chief up on charges. That dirt should have been cleaned up before the plane was okayed to fly."

"Well it's sort of your own God damn fault, you know."

"Okay, tell you what. I won't bring charges against the crew chief, and maybe the next time you'll be flying that plane, and when the fuckin' prop falls off, you might want to file charges yourself."

There was a pause while my retort was digested, then Chester, whose nickname was Cheek, said, "You're right, Glenn. But you shoulda had your goggles on. If that happened at 5,000 feet, you'd be dead."

"I think we have a right to expect those planes to be perfect when we climb into the cockpit."

"You're fuckin' A we do," chimed in Whiskey, who had acquired his nickname because of his apparent hollow legs.

"And I'll tell you something else," I said. "I'm going to the squadron commander and registering a private complaint against Mac. He did a lousy job. I can't ever remember this squadron not hitting its assigned target. And not only that, we'll still have to go back and get those fuckin' guns."

We continued to sip our whiskey and think about the situation. Cheek broke the silence, "Did anyone see Bob go in?"

"No," I answered, "when the squadron assembled, he just wasn't there. When I got hit, my element leader was keeping his eyes on me. He called Mac and said I went down. About that time he was on his own bomb run. He didn't see Bob's plane go in. I tell ya, things were really fucked at that point."

"Jesus, I wonder what happened?"

"He must have been hit in the cockpit—didn't have a chance to get on the radio."

"Well shit, that's the way it goes."

We didn't mourn the missing pilot; you simply couldn't dwell on things like that. Once someone was gone, they were gone. If you started to think about them, you had to get control of yourself fast; no postmortems. As the song says, "You lived in fame or went down in flame," and that's the way it was.

I realized I'd had a very close call that day, and the major cause had been because of my own carelessness. Combat flying is absolutely unforgiving. If you make a mistake, you pay the price. I had fortunately been given a reprieve today. By now I was an experienced combat pilot and maybe too cocky and overconfident. I'd better pay close attention to the rules and find that fine line again between too hot and not hot enough.

Dissension such as this was never publicized, but it definitely existed. The squadron leader was held to high exacting standards, as well he should have been. In this case he had failed, and all of the pilots knew it. It couldn't be brushed under the rug; an accounting would have to be made. I reported my unhappiness to the squadron commander the next morning. He told me he would take care of it, and he did. Mac never led the squadron again.

The crew chief of the plane I flew was disciplined severely and so was the line chief and the engineering officer. Everyone involved in this incident had been careless—including me. I'd learned my lesson the hard way. I wanted to make damn sure everyone else had too.

# chapter 18

# A PARADOX

Anyone who said they loved to fly combat missions was crazy, and anyone who said they didn't like to fly combat missions was of equal status. The real truth depended on the circumstances; it was a love-hate relationship.

The plus side was the thrill of flying itself, controlling a powerful machine that was free to move through an ocean of air, playing tag with fluffy white clouds, and staring down from 25,000 feet to the checkerboard of life on the ground.

The P-47 Thunderbolt did not have the sleek graceful lines of the P-51 Mustang nor the elegance and sheer beauty of the P-38 Lightning. It was big, ugly, and vicious looking. It was a brute designed to kill, and when the mission was off the ground and the squadron assembled, drawn up in tight formation heading for the target, it was beautiful. You were the winged warrior—ready to meet your foe and vanquish him. Like the knights of old, in shining armor, you were the white light, going against the sons of darkness. The welfare of your country was first, yours second. If this was your day to die—so be it; it would be an honorable death; your name and your exploits would live on even if your seed would never come to fruition. When the actual combat began, the thrill was an unimaginable high. The smell of gun smoke, the flak bursting all around you, the look and smell of the battlefield, your bombs and machine gun bullets tearing the enemy apart—it was the thrill of combat—and nothing in the life experience could come close to it. You were defending your family, your tribe, your clan, and the primal brain was screaming—KILL—KILL—KILL. You loved it.

On the minus side there was the ever-present thought that you might be killed. I don't want to die. I have too much to live for. I love my mom and dad; they'll be devastated if I die. I want to see my friends back home again, dance to Glenn Miller and Tommy Dorsey, take a girl to the beach at night and explore her lovely, naked body, hold her close, and enjoy the rapture of physical love.

At briefing when the target is announced, your guts flip, and when you hear what the predicted flak at the target will be, your heart pounds. Christ! You know what it's like; you've been there before. At takeoff your legs are shaking, but you're in the cockpit, and it's your turn to go—so you go. At the target you see the big, ugly burst of the 88s with the fireball center, and your plane is bucked from side to side as you wade through it. On the dive-bomb run you see the deadly stream of the quadmount 20s like a fire hose spraying the sky, and you have to go through it to get to the target. Your mouth is dry; you're scared shitless but keep on going. How could anybody love this. It's a trip through hell, and you hate it.

You must reconcile these diverse emotions; you must keep things in their proper perspective, and then you hear the strains of the song you sang in cadet school, "We live in fame or go down in flame for nothing can stop the Army Air Corps."

On the way back to the field there is a feeling of joy. The adrenaline is still flowing. You killed those Heinie bastards, and the war is that much closer to being won. At critique you brag about what you destroyed. That night you're drinking with your friends, rehashing all the details of the day's mission, realizing you're with the greatest bunch of bastards on the face of the earth and that you're living an experience few are privileged to know.

I never heard any pilot say he regretted killing Germans or that he was ashamed of what he was doing. This was war, and war is the business of killing. The faster we killed Germans, the sooner the war would end, then all the killing would stop, both German and American, and we could return to a normal life. But could we ever be like we were before? Hardly—even if not one drop of your blood was shed, the scars of war are permanent.

# chapter 19
# THE CHANGING FACE OF WAR

The war kept grinding on; our ground forces were moving ever closer to Germany itself, and the fighter-bomber groups had moved as well to new fields closer to the front lines.

But something else was changing; the Germans were adapting new tactics, and they had a telling effect. Some were psychological; others were physical. We were called to a pilots' meeting and presented with some bizarre facts; it was the intelligence department's assessment of Germany's latest weapons. The squadron intelligence officer began the briefing.

"Gentlemen, Germany is losing the war, but they've got a lot of punch left. We now have detailed information on a series of new weapons. They don't seem to be designed to kill you, just unnerve you."

With this statement he had our undivided attention.

"The first is what we call spider flak. It's a shell fired from either 88s or 155s and is designed to produce a giant fireball and explosion. Then stuff falls out of it, debris floats around, and tendrils begin to drop from the main black cloud; that's why we call it spider flak. It's been described as looking just like a P-47 that got a direct hit and exploded, and as near as we know, there's no shrapnel; all its energy is in the explosion and smoke cloud. We think it's strictly a psychological weapon designed to unnerve you. Has anyone seen it?"

There was silence for a moment, and then someone said, "Yeah, I saw it on yesterday's mission. There was some flak at three o'clock, the other side of Yellow flight, but not close enough to worry about, and then this big explosion. I thought somebody had caught a midair, but I still saw four planes."

"I saw it too."

"Me too," someone else added.

He looked us all over like a teacher about to chastise his errant students, "Yet none of you reported it—why not?

"Cheek, you saw it. Why didn't you report it?"

"Shit," Cheek answered, "the whole fuckin' squadron saw it, except maybe Red flight. They were ahead of it."

"But you saw it and didn't report it—why?"

"Well—God damn it, Captain. When I first saw it, I figured somebody in Yellow flight had taken a direct hit and blew up, but Yellow flight still had four planes. By that time that black shit was way behind us. Nobody called it out, and by then I wasn't sure what the hell I saw. I figured at critique one of the flight leaders would report it, but nobody said anything about it, so I shut up."

He kept his stern expression, "Has anyone anything to add?"

Someone in the back of the room spoke up, "I can tell you one thing; it sure as hell looks like somebody got hit and blew up, and if it's supposed to unnerve us, it sure as hell unnerved me."

To see a plane explode in midair, bombs and all, causes a terrible psychological impact. Sure, you see guys go in and explode when they hit the ground or lose half a wing and spin in out of control, but there's always the chance they got out, even if you didn't see a chute. But to see a plane flying along and suddenly explode is awful. There's just no airplane left, just little pieces falling away from the fireball. It's the worst possible thing to see.

"All right. We'll move on to the next one."

I had an idea what might be coming, and I hoped for my own sanity that he'd describe what I had seen twice.

"We call this one Bubbles, and the only thing we know about it is all of a sudden your plane is surrounded by clear globes—bubbles—about the size of grapefruit, and just as suddenly as they appear, they disappear. Has anyone seen these?"

Jim and I looked at each other. I had seen them a week or so ago on two separate occasions and had told him about it, making him promise not to say anything to anyone, but as yet, he had not seen them.

"Yes, sir," I said. "I've seen them twice, but they're not all the same size bubbles. Some are as large as volleyballs."

"And, of course, you reported it."

"Huh! You know damn well I didn't."

"Why not?"

"I'll tell you why, Captain. In the first place if I'd uv reported that to you, you wouldn't uv believed it; nobody else in the squadron said anything about being surrounded by transparent balls, and in the second place you'd uv told the flight surgeon, and he'd uv grounded me and maybe sent me to a fuckin' nut house."

There were a few laughs, and then things settled down again. He wanted some information on them.

"Tell me what you saw."

"Well, I remember I was under 2,000 feet. We were trying to find some targets of opportunity when all at once I ran into these balls. They were perfectly round and clear. I could see them streaming past the canopy and over the top of the wings. Scared the hell outta me. I figured it was some new kinda weapon and all those bastards would explode at once and I'd be in the middle of it."

"What did you do?"

"Kicked on 100 percent oxygen, figured maybe I was seeing things, but then they were gone, just like that. I looked around. Everybody was in formation.

Nobody said anything. Then I started to worry, maybe it was my imagination. And yes, it sure as hell unnerved me."

"And that's just exactly what we think they're designed for. How many of you have seen these?" About a third of the hands went up.

He began again, "We have one more to go. It seems they have some kind of a radio transmitter that's tied into their radar. It's been reported that suddenly you'll pick up a low hum in your headset. This hum will grow louder and higher pitched, and about the time it's screaming you'll get the first burst of flak. Has anyone experienced this?"

There was moaning and groaning, everyone talking at once. It was obvious that everyone had experienced it. One of the new guys said, "When I first heard it, I looked around, and the whole squadron was bobbing up and down."

Someone answered him, "That was everyone tucking in their asshole getting ready for the first burst."

"Yeah, tuck in real hard. It might keep the flak from going up your butt."

There followed a general discussion about these seemingly nonlethal but psychologically destructive weapons. Finally the squadron commander called for order. We quieted down in a hurry, and he stood there looking us all over.

"I want this clearly understood by every pilot in this squadron. You are to immediately report anything you encounter out of the ordinary, and I mean anything. I'm not picking on anyone. I'm as guilty as the rest of you, but from now on, anything strange, anything unusual, gets reported."

His eyes swept every pilot. He was serious, and we knew it.

"Does everyone understand that?"

There was a chorus of, "Yes, sir."

On our way out of the briefing room someone said, "Can you imagine those bastards wasting all that effort on that shit; no wonder they're losing the war."

"Yeah," came the reply, "but it sure had us fucked up for awhile."

There were some other developments as well, but they weren't brought up in the meeting; however, they were no secret. We had noticed that of late the flak was being concentrated on a single plane rather than the entire squadron. This didn't always happen, but it did enough to recognize it as a change in tactics.

It generally appeared that each gunner would pick a plane on his own and shoot at it. Sometimes he wouldn't follow you out of the target but break off and direct his fire at another incoming plane. This new tactic was different. All the guns firing would shoot at the same plane. This was controlled, concentrated fire, and when they employed it, it was deadly. But we surmised they would have to have a fire control center to employ this method, and that was not possible at all times.

Our counter tactic was to come to the aid of that plane by attacking the guns, but it wasn't always successful. It was just part of the perfection being achieved by both sides in the business of killing. But the improvements were not all on their side.

There were two constant problems for the fighter-bomber pilot. One was to locate and identify the specific target the ground troops wanted destroyed; the other was to identify our own troops so that we would not mistakenly attack them. We had gained a great deal of experience in both of these areas since D-Day.

As far as identifying enemy targets, the biggest breakthrough came when we put Thunderbolt pilots with the ground troops to act as forward controllers. The ground guys had done a good job, but not good enough; after all, they were either infantry or armor, but they were not pilots. Many mistakes resulted from faulty ground control because the controller just couldn't visualize the target or the problems in finding it from the fighter-bomber pilot's perspective. After much complaining on the part of both pilots and ground troops, someone in higher command began to get the message—put a fighter-bomber pilot on the ground, at the front, with an aircraft radio, and let him guide the planes to the target. Forward air controller teams were formed that consisted of a pilot, three enlisted men, and a radio equipped jeep. Sometimes the radio was transferred to a tank or other armored vehicle, and the pilot worked from there. This was a real breakthrough and gave the pilots much more confidence, knowing there was an experienced fighter-bomber pilot giving them direction from the ground. But what happened if that pilot was captured and the radio fell into the hands of the Germans? Well, it happened. But we still had an ace in the hole; it was the Authenticator. This was simply a code of letters and numbers. Any time the pilot in the air became suspicious of the instructions he was receiving from the ground, he would, without preamble, give his half of the code. If the ground controller didn't respond immediately with the other half of the code, the pilot would cuss him out, tell him to go to hell, and totally disregard his directions. Even if the ground controller did respond with the correct code and the pilot was still suspicious, he would question him about his background. It would sound like this over the radio:

Ground controller: "There is a wooded area full of German troops just south of your position. Please attack them."

Pilot: "There is more than one wooded area. Which one? Zebra 472."

Ground controller: "What?" (He should have said, "Say again.")

Pilot: "Zebra 472."

Ground controller: "I didn't get that, but attack now; we need your help."

Pilot: "Listen you Heinie bastard. Get off the radio."

Or if the ground controller came back with the right code response, which would have been another letter with three numbers and the pilot was still suspicious, it might sound like this:

Pilot: "Where you from in the States?"

Ground controller: "Los Angeles."

Pilot: "How far is that from Frisco?"

Ground controller: "Oh, I can't remember. I've never been there."

Pilot: "Get off the radio you Heinie bastard."

Ground controller: "No, I'm an American, and I've got a target for you; we need you bad—right now."

Pilot: "Sing Mairzy Doats" (pronounced Mare-Zee-Dotes, which was a super popular song that every G.I. from Europe to the Pacific knew by heart).

Ground controller: "What?"

Pilot: "Listen you Heinie son-of-a-bitch. Get off the radio."

The authenticator was changed daily, and if it was used during a mission, it was considered invalid for the rest of that day.

Of course the Germans were listening to every word we said over the radio. Sometimes we would call for smoke to be placed on the target so that we could make positive identification. Occasionally the Germans would oblige and shoot their smoke shells, placing them on our troops. This did result in attacks on our own troops by fighter-bombers, but our ground commanders were quick to counter this very clever German tactic. Regular smoke was out; from then on it was colored smoke, and just to make doubly sure, two colors would often be used. After the smoke shells were fired our ground controller would say over the radio, "Smoke is on the way." He would then wait a few seconds and just before the shells hit would say, "The smoke is red and green." We would watch, and there would be red smoke and a few seconds later green smoke. That was a positive identification, and the timing was such that the Germans couldn't get in on the act.

We often hit targets that were not much more than the length of a football field, or less, in front of our troops. This was hairy stuff. To keep from killing our own troops they would use 3x5-foot colored panels made of oilcloth. Of course these could be captured, so again, a color scheme was used. Our troops would display the panels, arranged by the color that had been designated for that day. The panels would mark their front line position, and anything forward of that panel was enemy. The same system was used by tanks and other armored vehicles. They'd simply drape the colored panel over their vehicle to identify themselves as American. This system was simple and effective, and as far as I know, the Germans were never able to compromise it.

# chapter 20

# BLACKOUT

All combat flying was physically demanding but particularly so for the fighter-bomber pilot. On very heavily defended targets it was not unusual to go in from 25,000 feet or higher. From this extreme height it was easy to attain a speed of 500 miles per hour in the dive. Pulling out of that dive would exert about five (or more) Gs on the pilot, resulting in a complete blackout. This physical experience was correctly named, because you saw black.

On the downward leg of the dive there were minor physiological changes in blood flow due to inertia. This resulted from accelerating from 250 miles per hour (speed at the beginning of the dive) to 500 miles per hour (speed attained just before pullout).

Gravitational force is always toward the center of the earth; in the dive the plane and pilot were flowing with that force going in that direction, so no Gs were felt. G is an expression of gravitational forces on the body. As you sit in your favorite chair reading or watching television, you are experiencing a 1 G force. That is equivalent to the mass of your body (weight) exerted against the earth. A 2 G force is double that, a 3 G force triple, and so on up the scale. A pilot weighing 150 pounds experiencing 5 Gs in a pull-out is experiencing the pressure of 5 times his body weight exerted on him—or 750 pounds. If your hand is pulled away from the throttle or the stick or a foot slips off a rudder pedal, there is no way you're going to get it back there until the G force returns to near normal. So this extreme force plasters your butt to the seat and your feet to the floor. But what about your insides?

The blood flowing throughout your body moves within a free-flowing self-contained system and is completely subject to the laws of gravity. As the plane is pulled out of the dive, the blood responds to this and flows down, which is away from the head. As the blood leaves the head (brain), vision becomes impaired. A darkness appears in your peripheral vision and very rapidly closes in. In a matter of a second or two you can only see the wing tips, then just the instrument panel, finally a single instrument, and then nothing. A good comparison can be gained by looking through an iris diaphragm; you'll find one in your camera. As you change the lens setting, the aperture closes leaving a smaller and smaller hole for the light to enter. Finally you can't see anything through the lens; it's blacked out.

The worst of the effects are felt after passing the horizontal as you begin to climb. Experience teaches you to relax the pull on the stick at this point just before reaching full blackout. You'll have absolutely no visual reference, and you're momentarily unconscious. If you continue backward pressure, when you wake up and can see again, you'll find yourself going straight up, and in those days even a Thunderbolt wouldn't last long in that angle of climb without stalling or spinning out, either of which could be deadly.

A blackout or semi-blackout could be repeated several times during a mission, but there didn't seem to be any adverse physical effects with the exception of a headache. Headgear was primitive in those days. Helmets, oxygen masks, and ear phones all fit tightly against the face and head, so most likely they were the prime cause. I can recall severe face and head pain after missions that did not involve blackouts, so most of us didn't consider the unconsciousness damaging, just annoying.

There were other physiological problems. Atmospheric pressure at sea level is 14.7 pounds per square inch. At 25,000 feet this pressure is reduced to about 4.5 pounds per square inch The inside and outside pressure of the body cavities would be the same prior to takeoff. As you gained altitude, the outside pressure would reduce. In most cases the inside pressure would do the same to maintain an equilibrium. Every once in awhile, the inside and outside pressure would equalize all at once. You have experienced this driving up a mountain. You will feel a pressure build-up inside your ears, then they will pop, and the pressure is equalized. But the real problem involved internal gases. Some of this gas would be expelled, but much remained trapped in the intestines. As altitude increased, the outside pressure decreased causing the trapped gas to expand. It was not unusual for the stomach to stretch a couple of inches. Anything restricting this expansion would cause intolerable pain. Generally, during briefing we'd be told if we were going in at a high altitude; if so, as soon as the pilot got into the cockpit he'd unbuckle his belt and unbutton his pants, shorts, and shirt. The flight suit itself was loose fitting, so that was not a problem. Occasionally a mission that was planned for 10,000 feet would end up at 27,000 feet because of bad weather. In that case, at the first opportunity, you held the stick with your knees and loosened your clothing as fast as possible. I will add that altitude up to 20,000 feet presented no discomfort, but from there up, the discomfort factor increased rapidly.

Lack of oxygen, or anoxia, will eventually result in unconsciousness. It is insidious, so early detection was really the only countermeasure. Wearing the oxygen mask was mandatory at all times. It connected to the helmet and also contained the microphone. A flexible hose connected it to the oxygen supply on board the airplane. There was a regulator in the system that controlled the ratio of oxygen to outside air the pilot was breathing. At sea level it delivered 100 percent outside air (the oxygen content of air at sea level is approximately 22 percent, nitrogen 77 percent, other gases 1 percent). At 10,000 feet the regulator provided 100 percent pure oxygen.

All aviation cadets had training in the altitude chamber. Part of that training was to stay at 18,000 feet without oxygen for 15 minutes while giving written answers to questions from the instructor. The cadet then put on his oxygen mask, which was delivering 100 percent oxygen, and after two minutes read what he had written. In my case the answers were all incomplete, or I had answered the questions in an incorrect order. The most obvious thing was the size of the letters and spacing of words. It looked like a child's first attempt at writing, and all the while I thought I was doing an excellent job. The purpose of this exercise was to prove to the cadet that he was in the incipient stages of anoxia without realizing or recognizing it.

While climbing to high altitude there was no mechanical way to check your oxygen delivery system, but there was a way to find out if your body was oxygen deprived. We called it the C.T.F., which stood for Check The Fingernails—Count To Five. In the earliest stages of anoxia the lips and fingernails turn blue. So during the climb, once you passed 15,000 feet you did the C.T.F. We always wore gloves; first, because it was cold at any altitude over 8,000 feet, and second, because regulations and good sense required all parts of the body to be covered for protection in the event of an explosion in the cockpit. The layered technique for keeping warm was known in those days, so we had, as standard flying equipment, a pair of silk gloves, chamois gloves, and fur liner leather gloves. Now, this would be a bit much to remove all three and replace them every 60 seconds—you performed the C.T.F. that often—so we just used the leather glove on the right hand. This was the routine. If during briefing you were told the squadron would attack from 27,000 feet, you automatically knew the target was going to be very heavily defended, and it would be a 100 percent oxygen mission. Once in the cockpit, before you strapped in, you'd unzip your flying suit, unbuckle your belt, unbutton your pants, shorts and shirt, then zip up your suit. You'd tuck your right-hand silk and chamois glove in your right knee pocket and tighten your oxygen mask straps. Now you were ready.

As you crossed 16,000 feet, you'd glance at the clock on the instrument panel, and when the sweep second hand was straight up, you'd hold the stick with your knees, put your right hand under your left armpit and pull your hand free. While counting from one to five, you'd closely examine your fingernails. A nice pink color signaled an all-clear so back with the hand to the armpit where the glove was being held, slip it into the glove, and grab the stick. This entire procedure took six to seven seconds. You were okay now until the second hand was straight up again, and you'd repeat this procedure three or four times. The procedure would be repeated when you hit 18,000 feet and again at 20,000. By then you were assured your oxygen system was doing what it was supposed to do—keeping you alive in a hostile environment.

One major physical problem was the susceptibility to what was called aerotitus—the medical term for blown eardrums. Pressure on the outside of the eardrum had to equal the pressure on the inside of the eardrum, or injury to the delicate membrane would result. At 27,000 feet the pressure was about three-pounds per square inch. The pilot begins his attack by doing a wing-over and heads straight down. By the time he gets through this rolling turn and into the dive, he's going 375 miles per hour; 15 seconds later as he crosses 18,000 feet, he's going 450 miles per hour, and the outside pressure on his eardrums has doubled since he began the dive.

He eases the dive angle to 30 degrees as he crosses 10,000 feet and is now heading straight for the target. He holds his speed at 450 miles per hour—bomb release is 20 seconds away—and at that point the outside pressure on his ears is nearly 15 pounds per square inch.

During the entire dive, which has taken less than 60 seconds, the pressure on the inner eardrum has equalized constantly, so no discomfort has been felt or injury incurred. But what happens if the Eustachian tube (a small tube running from the inner ear to the throat) is swollen or irritated from a head cold and does not allow the rapid passage of pressure? In that case the ear drum ruptures, which is accompanied by excruciating pain. This did not relieve the pilot of his mission objective. It was his duty to attack and destroy the target as long as he was still alive and conscious, so he must complete his bomb run, release his bombs on the target, and fly all the way back to his base before he could get any relief from the pain. There was nothing that could be done anyway except nose drops to hopefully lessen the swelling of the Eustachian tube and allow the pressure to equalize. However, the damage was already done; the pain remained but by now had lessened to the level of an abscessed tooth. The pain was usually gone in three days, but the pilot should not fly for at least two weeks. We rarely had the leeway of that much time for recovery, so every effort was made to schedule that pilot for a low level mission.

You must remember in those days there were no pressurized cockpits, so the physical abuse to the pilot was, in many cases, quite severe. We were introduced to G suits in July of 1944, but they were so cumbersome and ineffective that we refused to wear them. Fortunately they were improved and later became standard wear for fighter and fighter-bomber pilots, but that did not happen until after the war was over. But due to man's great ingenuity, they were ready for the next war.

## chapter 21

# FRIENDLY FIRE

The stupid jerk who came up with that euphemism probably got a medal. It means being fired on by your own side, but in reality it means being killed by your own people. There is nothing FRIENDLY about that. It is mistaken fire, caused by lack of combat experience, bad intelligence information, trigger-happy soldiers who are scared, or improper identification. No matter the reason, it is a mistake of the highest magnitude because it means Americans have killed Americans or Allied Forces have killed Allied Forces.

The Gulf War brought this unfortunate experience into the living rooms of America, and we were aghast, but friendly fire was not unique to the Gulf War. Stonewall Jackson was a victim in the Civil War, killed by his own sentry; it happened in World War I and during World War II; it struck privates and generals alike. Lieutenant General (three star) Lesley J. McNair, Chief of the Army Ground Forces, was killed in France when bombs from B-17s of the Eighth Air Force fell short of their target.

Although the circumstances surrounding a soldier's death by friendly fire are usually covered up or at least not publicized, it was not an unusual event. The incident is always thoroughly investigated, but to my knowledge, at least, no action has ever been taken against those involved.

I'll relate some instances, and you be the judge as to the guilt or innocence of the parties. These episodes are described accurately to the best degree possible, but getting both sides of the story is understandably difficult or impossible. I'm being purposely vague about the time and place of these events out of respect for the people or units involved, but to my personal knowledge, these events did occur.

A group of Thunderbolts, armed with 500-pound bombs, were proceeding to a target. They were under the direction of mission control, which was called Joint Operational Control (J.O.C.), air and ground personnel sitting around tables with maps keeping track of the progress of the group; the main controller was in constant voice contact with the aircraft.

The weather had been marginal, and it was not certain if the target area would be clear, but the Thunderbolts were heading for it anyway, flying at about 20,000 feet, which was about 5,000 above the top of the cloud cover. As the mission progressed, it became clear to the controller, based on the reports he received, that the target would be socked in, and because the weather in the entire area was the same, it was decided to abort the mission rather than go to an alternate target. There was no point in losing valuable pilots and planes to bad weather if it could be avoided.

Once the decision had been made at the J.O.C., the controller immediately called the group leader and told him to return to base. The group leader acknowledged that order and in turn gave his order to the group to jettison their bombs because they were returning to base. One quick-thinking squadron commander immediately ordered his squadron to hold their bombs, but the two other squadrons complied and 48 500-pound bombs (two bombs per plane, 12 planes per squadron) went sailing toward the ground.

While the plane is on the ground, the bombs are attached to a shackle on the underside of the wing. The fuse is then screwed into the front of the bomb; sometimes a tail fuse is also used. On the tip of the fuse is a small propeller, and a wire is inserted through that propeller and attached to the shackle. As long as that propeller is in the front of the fuse, the bomb is unarmed. To arm it, the pilot pulls a lever inside the cockpit, which secures the wire to the shackle, and when the bomb is released it falls free of the plane, but the wire remains with the plane. Now the propeller is free to rotate, and it does as the wind moves over the nose of the bomb. A few rotations and the propeller separates from the fuse, and the bomb is armed and will explode on contact.

When bombs were jettisoned, they were dropped unarmed with the wire still attached to the fuse propeller. In theory they would not explode when they hit the ground, but occasionally they did. In this case the majority did not, but a few did.

The mission had been planned so that at least half of the flight plan was over friendly territory. At the midway point, the group would turn east and very shortly be over enemy territory heading for the target. The quick-thinking squadron commander who told his squadron to hold their bombs was aware that he was still on the leg of the flight over friendly territory.

Unfortunately, when the group, or rather the two squadrons of the group, jettisoned their bombs they were over a rear rest area, and many infantry soldiers became casualties due to friendly fire.

Who is to blame for such a catastrophe? The controller gave the order to abort the mission and return home. This automatically meant that the bombs would be jettisoned, but he could not give that order; that would be up to the group leader. The group leader gave the order to jettison but did not realize he was still over friendly territory. Remember the group was flying above the overcast and had not seen the ground since shortly after takeoff. He was preoccupied with the mission. He had the responsibility of getting 36 aircraft and pilots ready to do battle, of getting them in the air precisely when he was ordered to do so. His concern now was the possibility that he would have to find a target obscured by bad weather, attack it successfully, and get his group back to their base and probably face horrible landing conditions—again due to bad weather. He certainly had many things on his mind.

# CHAPTER 21: FRIENDLY FIRE

The group leader is also the leader of the first squadron. The second squadron leader did not countermand the group leader's order to jettison the bombs; he simply obeyed the order as did the other pilots in those two squadrons. Counting all personnel, there were about 60 people involved, 36 pilots, plus 24 at the J.O.C. Yet only one person was aware of the possible lethal effects of jettisoning bombs at that particular moment.

Inside the J.O.C. there is a big plot board. All ground units, both friendly and enemy, are identified and located on this plot board. As the mission progresses, a symbol representing the group in the air is pushed along the flight path, which is drawn on the plot board. In some cases the plot was accurate; in others it was an educated guess. It all depended on the radar and direction-finding equipment in use at that time. Remember we're talking 1944 here, and those things were quite primitive then.

In the chapter on POWs you read about several Americans who died as a result of strafing by American aircraft. It happened deep in Germany; the American prisoners were in a German truck headed for a POW camp. The aircraft overhead spotted the German truck column and attacked, which is exactly what they were supposed to do—not knowing, of course, that there were American prisoners aboard.

It was not just soldiers on the ground who were killed by friendly fire; it also worked in reverse. During the drive into Germany, each small village or town was defended by the retreating Germans. Maybe retreating is not the correct word; they were being beaten back, village by village, town by town, and the fighting was fierce.

The air-ground combination was at its best under this type of fighting; it worked like this: The ground forces would start an attack, and when they ran into heavy resistance, they would call for air support. The Thunderbolts that were on station near by would come in and attack the enemy armor and troops holding the town, and when they figured they'd killed them off or neutralized them, they'd pull off and tell the ground boys to go ahead. There could still be isolated pockets of stiff resistance, so the Thunderbolts would hang around for awhile until the air-ground controller told them they were no longer needed. The air-ground controller would be a Thunderbolt pilot temporarily assigned to the ground unit so he would be right with the troops and had a first-hand knowledge of the situation.

When the Thunderbolts pulled off, they'd usually fly back to the last town that had been captured. This would give the pilots a temporary break from enemy fire, and also, if they had been hit and had to bail out, they would be over friendly territory. In addition they would be close by, on call, if they were needed.

This leapfrog situation had been working very effectively at that stage of the war when one day things went wrong. A flight of Thunderbolts had attacked a village successfully and turned it over to the ground troops. They then flew about five miles to the rear over a town that had been taken the day before.

After strenuous fighting, when you get back to friendly territory you can relax, circle slowly, and wait for your next call. The flight had just started to orbit over this town at about 700 feet when the ground troops opened fire. One pilot must have been killed in the cockpit because his plane just went straight into the ground and exploded. Another was shot up quite badly but managed to make it back to the base. The other two planes in the flight were not hit. The entire incident didn't last over 10 seconds. The result was one American pilot killed, one plane lost, and another badly damaged. The troops responsible had just been moved into this position and had not yet tasted combat. They claimed they had been strafed by Thunderbolts earlier in the day and weren't taking any chances and decided to fire when the Thunderbolts started to circle.

Now if you were sitting on a board of inquiry to determine responsibility and punishment—how would you judge the people involved in these tragic events?

I had two friendly fire personal experiences that were near-disasters. We were returning from a mission, and it was nearly dark. Because we were over friendly territory, the squadron was flying in regular formation. All at once we came under severe attack by our own antiaircraft. They were shooting radar-directed, 90-millimeter flak. It was plenty close, but no one was shot down. We probably took some hits, but we had battle damage already from our target. Anyway, a hole is a hole, and there's no way to tell by looking whether it was made by German or American flak. The event was explainable; the J.O.C. had failed to clear us through our own antiaircraft positions along our route home to base. Thunderbolts did not usually fly at night, so anything in the air was presumed enemy. The antiaircraft boys had a perfect right to fire. That's what they were supposed to do.

The other experience was horrible. I was leading my flight looking for targets of opportunity; that meant anything you could find to shoot at. We were well into enemy territory, at least according to our briefing that morning. I spotted a column of armored vehicles and trucks from about 5,000 feet. I told my flight we would attack line abreast and then go into a strafing pattern, each plane taking the next vehicle in line. This was a standard, and usually successful, attack plan.

I peeled over from 5,000 feet and started in to the center of the column where there were trucks full of soldiers. It was standard practice for the flight leader to remind his flight to arm their guns, which I did as I started the dive. I was waiting for the antiaircraft fire to come up, but it didn't. At about 1,000 feet I was ready to open fire when I suddenly realized I was looking at a star on the side of the truck, and the men in the truck were waving, not shooting. I immediately yelled into the radio,"Hold your fire. They're American!" By now I was just pulling up over them and shaking like a leaf.

I circled around, put the flight in trail, and flew alongside of them in their same direction about 10 feet above the ground. This way they could see me waving to them and waggling my wings. I told the rest of the flight to do the same.

I was so shook-up I headed straight for home and kept saying over and over again, "You stupid son of a bitch, you nearly killed those guys." After we landed I asked the other members of the flight if they recognized the column as American, and not one of the other pilots did. Why? Because we were well into enemy territory far beyond the point where American troops were supposed to be according to our briefing that morning, and the column was heading east just as every other retreating German column was doing; and most important of all, they were not displaying any color identification panels.

I'll bet the G.I.s in those trucks have told that story to their grandchildren, and it was only by a split second that they lived at all. How would I have felt if I'd opened fire and my flight had done the same? We would have killed a lot of Americans, and I would have been responsible.

I'll tell you one thing; I couldn't drink enough booze that night to drive that image from my mind, and I'm not ashamed to say I wasn't worth a damn for a week. It's not just the incident that works its havoc. I found myself taking too much time in order to positively identify a vehicle as enemy before ordering an attack or opening fire. This increased the risk to myself and the other members of my flight. When I realized this, and this realization was probably prompted by hints from my wing man and element leader, I had to face the fact that it could happen again, but that could not be an excuse for lessening my aggressive performance. I personally never gave a second thought about killing Germans, nor did I ever hear any of the other pilots express any remorse. They were Germans; they were the enemy, and we were there to kill them, but the thought of killing an American damn near became an obsession. This was a hazard of war that could not be conceived of during training, but it was there when you went into combat, and you had to live with it.

# chapter 22

# TWELVE O'CLOCK HIGH

There was no mission scheduled, and we were lolling around waiting for something to happen. Shortly it did. There was an urgent meeting called for all pilots. It was being held in the briefing room, a place all too familiar to us.

After we were seated, wondering what was about to happen, the squadron commander opened by saying there was disturbing news about a new type of aircraft the Germans had perfected, and it could have an effect on the outcome of the war. With this, he turned it over to the intelligence officer. We had noticed something on the wall that was covered with a sheet. The intelligence officer, with all the drama of a Mickey Mouse cartoon, dropped the covering and displayed a silhouette drawing of a very strange looking aircraft. He announced it was a German "jet." We asked what a jet was, and he told us it was a new type of propulsion engine that drove the plane, but it didn't use a propeller. "How does it fly without a propeller?" we asked. "It just farts its way through the air," he replied. We were then briefed on its speed and flying characteristics, and when we heard it had a cruising speed of 500 miles per hour, we were damned concerned. Where was our jet? If we were winning the war and if our aircraft builders, our war department people, and the Army Air Corps were so damn good, where was our jet fighter?

Two weeks later we were on a mission looking for German fighters. It was rumored the Luftwaffe was finally coming up to tangle with the fighter-bombers boys, and we were ecstatic. No bombs to weigh us down, just a belly tank to give us more time in the air, and we'd drop the tank the moment we engaged the German fighters.

This was a "full strength" mission, meaning we had four flights instead of the usual three. When we flew this configuration, the squadron was split into two boxes of two flights each. Our regular squadron commander was leading the squadron. I was leading the second box. He was an excellent pilot, and we all hoped he'd find the elusive Luftwaffe. Our ground controller had, so far, sent us on a couple of wild goose chases and now gave us a new heading supposedly to intersect a flight of German fighters; we were at 12,000 feet. The squadron commander made a gentle right turn to take up the new heading, and I slid the box under him intending to take up position on his left side and a little above him. This would be an advantageous place to be in the event of an attack on the squadron from enemy fighters.

The hour numbers on the clock face were used to indicate relative directions.

For example, if another plane was at three o'clock, that meant it was directly to your right; if it was at six o'clock, it was directly on your rear. High, low, and level completed the location descriptions, so if a plane was at twelve o'clock high, it meant the plane was directly ahead of you but higher than you were.

Anyway, I moved the box over, and as I cleared the last man in the first box, I began a gentle climb to gain some altitude and was still turning to maneuver into position. When you're climbing and turning, the airplane is in a nose-high attitude, so your forward visibility is reduced. At this point I caught a glint or reflection that just wasn't supposed to be there. I pushed the stick forward for a better look and there he was—one of the new ME 262 German jet fighters at twelve o'clock high and coming straight at me. His guns were firing—when you're looking straight at them they wink and blink, but that's no friendly salutation. I called his position immediately, gave my plane full war emergency power, and pulled the nose up so I could get into position to fire at him. However, he was coming too fast and was in too steep a dive, and my bullets passed harmlessly by him. In the next split second I feared a midair crash. He wasn't banking away; he was still heading straight at me. I called a break to the right hoping everyone could get out of his way in time. His speed was totally out of my perspective. I just couldn't comprehend another aircraft closing with me at that speed. As soon as I broke right, I broke left again, intending to follow him down or at least try to keep him in sight. As I was in that tight left turn, I saw him roll over on his back—as he would do if he intended to do a split S maneuver—and he was at less than 10,000 feet. He hit the ground a few seconds later; there was a big explosion and fireball and that telltale black, oily looking smoke that identifies a crash.

When he passed me, I got a fast glimpse of him in the cockpit; he was that close. What made him pull that stupid stunt? Was he showing off his new toy for us to see? One thing for sure is that he was disoriented as to his altitude; he probably thought he was at 20,000 feet. In that event he would have had ample room to roll over on his back, dive down, and pull up again. None of us hit him. The camera film later verified that—and by a miracle he didn't hit any of us. Because we didn't actually shoot him down, nobody could get credit for a "kill," even though that German pilot was as killed as anybody could get.

The rest of the mission was uneventful. We were put on course to intercept some enemy fighters, but as we closed in on them, they turned out to be English Spitfires. Later the same thing happened, but our quarry this time were P-51s. This is a hairy situation. The P-51, from certain angles, looked a great deal like a German Messerschmitt 109, and the P-47, again from certain angles, looked like a Focke-Wulf 190. When your controller is directing you into position and telling you you are about to intersect a group of enemy fighters, you naturally expect them to be enemy fighters. You first spot them at a distance and then move on in for the fight. They spot you and clearly see your aggressive action and under those circumstances, in the excitement and blood lust of a pending battle, you have all the makings of a tragic event—American fighters shooting down American fighters.

Fortunately we and they were able to identify in time to prevent an accidental shoot-out, but it was a close call.

We returned to our field feeling extremely disappointed. Here was our first chance to actually go out and look for German fighters, and we couldn't find any, except one who was dumb enough to kill himself. The next day it was back to the dirty work, the dive-bombing, strafing, and flak gun shoot-outs.

# chapter 23

# NOT ALL BAD

Combat flying produced a high degree of stress. There probably is nothing in life that could exceed it. Booze was the most effective relief, and we followed that prescription with great dedication. Heavy drinking was a daily affair. We usually finished our evening meal about 1800 hours and then got down to some serious drinking. We often combined the drinking with cards or a general bull session. Stress diminished in direct proportion to the amount of alcohol consumed. My circle of friends contained all cheerful drunks, so we had fun. If someone was depressed, the others cheered him up. Depression was something that led to certain death. Once a pilot was on that road, if he couldn't snap out of it, he was finished. This was an unspoken circumstance that we all understood.

We rarely got a night out; usually we were miles from a town, which presented transportation problems. Also, it must have been against Ninth Air Force policy to allow its precious pilots to run the risk of death or injury due to traffic accidents, especially when they'd be drunk at the time. On rare occasions we would get a night on the town, but generally under supervision. That meant the squadron commander would be present along with other senior squadron officers. That put a bit of a damper on things, but we still had fun.

One such excursion was to Brussels, Belgium. A rumor was floating around that in a certain cabaret "there was an entertainer who picked up cigarettes from the table top with her tits and could also hold a lighted cigarette in her pussy and make it puff." This we had to see and raised enough hell so that arrangements were finally made. About 20 of us went on the trip, which was damn near all the pilots we had left at that time.

It was early November and a very cold 40-minute ride to town; hopefully it would be worth it. One of the prerequisites for a job in this place as a waitress was a 40-inch bust line and a big ass. Europeans preferred that build.

After several rounds of drinks, some dancing and chit chat, the star performer finally made her appearance and opened her blouse.

"My God, look at those tits," someone said.

"Over here, baby. Lemme feel those things."

# CHAPTER 23: NOT ALL BAD

"Here's some American cigarettes honey. Come on and pick 'em up with those luscious boobs of yours."

She went from table to table bending down, pressing her tits together with her hands, scooping up cigarettes. It didn't demand a great degree of talent—but it was different. After some persuasion she finally lighted a cigarette, placed it on the corner of the table, lifted her dress, and worked herself over the unlit end. Sure enough, she was able to grasp it and move away from the table proudly displaying it in the grip of mother nature.

Everyone hooted and howled and called her from table to table. She'd pick the table with the biggest tip and go into her act again.

"Christ, have you ever seen anything like that in your life? Her pussy is smoking that Lucky."

Someone quietly said, "She's big as a cow."

"I think she's a slob," someone else answered.

"So who gives a shit. When's the last time you had a pussy that close to your face?"

"Speaking of pussy, let's haul ass outta here and go find some."

There was general support for this proposition, but we'd been drinking since dinner, and by then the brandy, on top of the whiskey we'd consumed on the way in, was beginning to take its toll. A couple of guys slid off their bar stools and peacefully rested on the floor, and a couple more fell over a table with the same result. Someone suggested we paint a target on the floor, stand on the bar, down a drink, and throw the empty glass at it; that would prove beyond doubt who the best fighter-bomber pilot was. That seemed to be the signal for the squadron commander, who was playing mother goose, to call it a night.

By the time we reached the base everyone, except mother goose, was passed out. Someone had the foresight to have some enlisted men standing by to help us to our quarters. Otherwise we'd all have frozen to death in the back of the trucks. Fortunately there was no mission the next day, so we were able to nurse our hangovers at a respectable pace. Incidentally, there was a divided opinion on whether the cigarette actually puffed or was content to just smolder in that most unusual cigarette holder.

The squadron photographer was along on that epic adventure and took lots of pictures of us gawking at that class act involving the cigarettes. We all got prints, but to my certain knowledge, no one sent them home—wouldn't want to spoil the image of that all-American, clean-cut, upstanding, church-going young man who made it through cadet school and was now a fighter-bomber pilot. The Army Air Corps preferred pictures of the pilots receiving holy communion or the blessings of the chaplain before they went on a mission. But as I said before, if you're going to tell the true story of the Fighter-Bomber Boys, you've got to tell it like it really was.

There is one thing that should be cleared up at this point. The pilots were allowed to drink as much as they wanted to, get as drunk as they wanted to, as long as it didn't affect their ability as a combat pilot. The mission schedule was put on the board in late afternoon for the next day. Takeoff time, if known, was also posted. In some cases the mission was off the ground at sunup or shortly afterwards, or it may not be until much later in the morning. Occasionally a mission could be delayed for a couple of days, due to weather, but in any event, you always knew when you were scheduled for the next mission the squadron would fly.

Although drinking was a nightly affair, it was absolutely prohibited during the daytime; if you were on the morning mission, you just got slightly drunk the night before. No pilot would risk his life flying with a full-blown hangover, and the other pilots wouldn't tolerate it. Flying combat required great skill and physical stamina, and both were impaired by too much booze the night before. Each pilot knew his limit, and I never saw anyone exceed what they could handle and still be in top shape for duty the next morning.

Now here we are, decades later, reading about a bunch of pilots getting smashed every night but only half smashed if they had to fly the next day. We are, in this day and age, aware of the airlines' prohibition regarding their pilots drinking within a certain number of hours before they fly. Obviously, even if you're just slightly drunk the night before, you might not be at 100-percent efficiency when you climb into the cockpit, so why was drinking allowed at all? Because there were other things to consider. The strain of combat eats at the mind. The longer you're at it the worse it becomes, and the worst part of the day is the night. Your dead friends visit you in your dreams; you're hit and on fire but can't get the canopy open to bail out; you awaken in a cold sweat, but staying awake is preferable to falling asleep again. Without a good night's sleep you're no good in the morning; so, a slightly drunken sleep is more therapeutic than spending the night afraid to go to sleep and counting the minutes until it's your time to go on another mission.

In training we used to get drunk every night and not worry about hangovers. If you were on the morning flight, the minute you got into the cockpit and hooked up, you'd turn on 100-percent pure-rich oxygen. By the time you started the engine, taxied out and got into position for takeoff, you were 80 percent cured. There was one other thing about that aspect of training; you were training to be a killer, and killers had to be tough. Drinking helped to promote that image. Training flights were nearly all just you and your plane; if you crashed there was no one else involved. But in combat you were part of a squadron, a member of the team, and you had responsibilities to that team. So there was a difference in the attitude toward drinking and flying in training, as opposed to combat.

# chapter 24
# THE CALL OF NATURE

Most missions lasted about two to three hours but on occasion were longer. What happens if you feel the call of nature during that time? The bomber boys told me they had a little pot for that purpose, but, of course, in a fighter plane there was no room for such a convenience. There was a pilot relief tube, however, and if you had to urinate, you could use that. As far as the other was concerned, if you couldn't hold it, you went in your pants.

One of the funniest things I ever witnessed happened while we were flying out of our field in Belgium. It was November, cold, with snow on the ground. We were all lined up on the taxiway, moving up to takeoff position, when one plane pulled out of line and parked off the taxiway; the pilot hurriedly got out. He pulled off his jacket, unzipped his flight suit, dropped his pants and shorts, squatted under the wing, and relieved himself. It was the fastest one on record because in the next instant he was pulling up his clothes, getting into his jacket and back into the plane. He still made the takeoff, although he was in last position, but at least he took off with empty bowels. An incident like this wasn't exactly what the Army Air Corps P.R. people considered a newsworthy event, so obviously such stories were never released.

Once you were in that airplane and off the ground, whatever came up, you had to handle it, even if it was the call of nature.

And while we're on this unpleasant subject, there is something else to mention. Occasionally a bout of diarrhea would hit some of the pilots. It could be stress induced, tainted food, or a flu bug. If it was really bad, naturally you couldn't fly, but it was the borderline case that presented the problem.

Most dive-bomb attacks produced about 4 to 5 Gs. One G force is equivalent to the weight of your body, 4 Gs four times that weight, so in a 4-G pull-out the force on the body of a pilot weighing 165 pounds was actually 660 pounds. Now if you have a slight case of diarrhea and the urge hits you, you might be able to hold it in under ordinary circumstances, but when you pull out of a 4-G dive, there is no way you can prevent the force on your bowels overcoming whatever counterforce you try to exert. One day I heard this on the radio:

"Bonebreak Yellow leader, this is Yellow three. I've got severe stomach cramps—all of a sudden. Just wanted you to know."

"Yellow three, do you want to abort?"

"Negative, Yellow leader. We're too close to the target. I'll stick it out."

Shortly after that conversation, the squadron arrived at the target and dive-bombed it. Yellow leader was concerned about his element leader (Yellow three), so after the pull-out he called him on the radio.

"Yellow three from Yellow leader. How you doin'?"

"Okay, Yellow leader—no more stomach cramps, but I could sure use a clean pair of shorts."

He had to sit in it all the way back. This story is a true account of the life of the fighter-bomber pilot. He ate, slept, got drunk, defecated, urinated, and got sex whenever he could. He was a living human being who had to deal with a most inhuman situation. Regardless of his superior abilities, his devotion to duty, and his nearly insane desire to acquire medals and become a hero, he was just like the average Joe—when he had to go—he had to go.

# chapter 25

# ROTATION

Up to now we had no plan of rotation, no idea what our tour of combat would be. The Eighth Air Force had a 25 mission limit on combat flying. After you made the magic 25 you were sent home, but you could volunteer for another tour. In most cases that request was granted, but you returned to the States first for a well-deserved extended leave.

When we first started flying combat, we were so eager to get into the war we didn't give much thought about how long we'd have to stay. We were also aware of the Eighth Air Force policy of 25 missions and just naturally assumed it would be the same in the Ninth. By now the old boys had far surpassed 25 missions and were voicing their displeasure about the no definite tour policy. Finally we had a visit from a general from Ninth Air Force Headquarters, and we figured we'd get the answer. One of the old boys was a big guy, very outspoken, and a career Army Air Corps officer. We were glad he'd be our spokesman. The meeting was held in the mess tent.

After the general addressed us and told us what a great job we'd been doing, our spokesman stood and addressed him, "General, we would like to know what our tour of duty is supposed to be." He then took his seat.

"Well, gentlemen," the general began, "our job is to support our ground forces, and there has been no actual tour of duty established. They have no tour of duty and, at this time, neither do we."

The captain stood again; even the other squadron senior officers were willing to let him handle it. "Sir, we are not in the ground forces. The Eighth Air Force has a tour of 25 combat missions. Many of us have already exceeded that number. What do we have to look forward to? The way things are now, we fly until we're killed or the war ends, and we have no idea when this war will end. We need to have something, General, some idea. If the Eighth has a definite tour, why don't we?"

There was immediate, verbal, unanimous support of his statement from the rest of the pilots. The general didn't appear too happy with the turn of events.

"Gentlemen, I have no authority to set a definite tour."

Our fearless spokesman pressed him on the issue, "Then who does, sir? There's no reason to treat us differently from the guys in the Eighth. And another thing,

General, my classmates who are flying with the Eighth, are all majors now. We're not getting the promotions that they are. We're all underranked and get damn little leave."

By now he continued to stand, and the meeting had turned into a test of wills between the captain and the general. It was obvious how it would turn out. Our squadron commander should have been our spokesman, but he had a personality problem. He had more guts than a slaughterhouse, was a really good combat pilot, but had absolutely no leadership ability, took little interest in the welfare of his pilots, and was probably scared of the general.

I got the distinct feeling that the general would give a lot if the captain would go away. I couldn't read his mind, but I felt he thought he'd just visit us, give us a snow job, pat us on the back, and everything would be okay, but it wasn't working out like that. There was hostility in the tent. He looked us over and said, "I'd like to know how the rest of you feel?"

This, of course, was a dismissal to the captain, but the ice had been broken, and now other flight leaders were willing to speak. The captain sat down.

Morgan, who was well liked and respected by all of us, took the floor.

"Sir, I believe all of us agree that we should have a definite tour of duty. As far as promotions go, if I was with the Eighth, I'd be a major now. Since I left England, I've had one leave and a three-day pass to Paris. I believe these things are very bad for morale. It's just not good. We're not getting a fair shake."

Others voiced their displeasure, and we knew the general got the message loud and clear. He ended the meeting with a promise.

"I will take your complaints to the commanding general, and I'm sure something will be done about it. I can't promise anything, but I'll do my best." With that the meeting ended, and we all left the mess tent and broke up into our private cliques.

There was no mission scheduled, so we went to our tent to talk about the meeting.

"Well, what do you guys think?"

# CHAPTER 25: ROTATION

"Think? Are you kiddin'? Nothing's gonna change. They've got us by the balls. Whata we gonna do, quit?"

"Yeah, let's just say, 'Well, General, I've flown enough for awhile. I think I'll take a vacation.'"

Why was this issue so important? There were many reasons. Your life was on the line every time you climbed into that cockpit. Sure you had courage, but how long could it last? Two months, six months, a year? As members of the squadron were killed off, you knew your chances of survival were diminishing. You wanted to be a combat pilot, but you also wanted to live, to return home and bask in the glory you so deserved. Each mission meant your chances of accomplishing that were that much less. Who knew when the war would end? Would we have any chance at all of surviving? There's no question that combat efficiency drops once a pilot begins to place his desire to live above the mission objective. A definite tour of duty offsets this because it gives him a goal. It worked great for the Eighth Air Force. It worked great for the navy who had the best system of all; they simply rotated the entire squadron after six months of combat. But in the Ninth Air Force, the Johnny Come Lately doing the dirty work was still being shortchanged, but things did change.

We never did get a definite tour established, but we did get something. As we received replacement pilots, the pilots with the most missions would be sent home. Of course this was predicated on the idea that we would get more pilots than we lost. But as it worked out, the flow of replacements increased—with the exception of some temporary lulls—and the first of the old boys went home.

We were encouraged by this, and the makeup of the squadron drastically changed. Eventually the number of replacement pilots outnumbered the original members. This made it a better squadron, with a few old boys, those of us who were some of the original replacements, and new eager pilots ready to test their guts and skills in the business of war.

## chapter 26

# BIG BATTLES

There were three decisive battles in the European war, and the outcome of each hung in the balance for awhile. Each had a major effect on the progress of the war, and even though the Allies demanded unconditional surrender, if Germany had won any of those battles, we may have had to settle for less.

The first was the D-Day Invasion. For 48 hours it was nip and tuck. Could we hold the beaches or would we be pushed into the sea?

The next was the Breakout at Saint-Lo. We had established a foothold but couldn't penetrate the tenacious German defensive positions. Would we end up in World War I-type trench warfare?

The third and last was the Battle of the Bulge. The Germans attacked, broke through our lines, and pushed our forces back for miles. There was no stopping them as day by day their juggernaut rolled on.

Regardless of their powerful offensive, it was too late for them to win the war, but their success threatened to prolong it indefinitely.

The Fighter-Bomber Boys were heavily engaged in all three battles, but the Battle of the Bulge proved beyond any question that the fighter-bomber was the weapon that tipped the scale.

Our airfield was near Brussels, Belgium, at that time. It was a former Luftwaffe base; the landing strip was blacktop and just over a mile long; it had a control tower, wide taxi-ways, and parking areas. Our quarters, about a mile away, were new, strafe-proof, red brick buildings with steam heat. We had an officers' club, a pilots' mess, and a large ready-room. The Luftwaffe went first class, and now we were reaping the benefit of it.

One morning in mid-December we woke up to zero-zero weather; actually we had a hard time finding our way to the pilots' mess for breakfast—it was that bad. We sure wouldn't be flying this morning. After breakfast we went to the regular morning briefing and were amazed at what we saw on the map. The Germans had attacked and broken through our front lines in several places. We figured that was no big deal because tomorrow, when the weather cleared and we could fly, we'd have a field day; they couldn't hide and attack at the same time. But it didn't work out that way.

# CHAPTER 26: BIG BATTLES

The German meteorologists had predicted the beginning of a weather phenomenon; zero-zero weather would keep every fighter-bomber group on the ground for more than a week, and the German high command decided this would be the perfect opportunity to attack in force and maybe change the outcome of the war.

The next day was the same; we couldn't fly. Each succeeding morning at briefing the story became more grim. The Germans were advancing, taking miles of territory each day, and our troops couldn't stop them. By the fourth day we were told we may have to abandon our airfield and retreat to France.

This was unacceptable to us. We weren't going to give this field up and go back to living in the mud. We'd figure out some way to save it. Phrases such as "withdrawing to a defensive position" or "dig in and hold" are not part of a fighter-bomber pilot's repertoire. He is trained to attack and attack and attack. Our ignorance of ground-to-ground fighting was pathetic, but in several meetings we decided we would not voluntarily leave.

Things were getting hectic by the seventh day. The Bulge on the map had reached well into Belgium. Other fighter-bomber groups were in the same boat. The decision was made to fly the airplanes out; they couldn't be allowed to fall into enemy hands. We would make an instrument takeoff and fly to other fields in France. If the weather there was closed down and we couldn't land, we'd stay up as long as possible hoping for a weather break; if it didn't, when the gas ran out, we'd have to bail out. How could this be happening? We're supposed to be winning the war.

About this time we were getting all kinds of reports about German soldiers in American uniforms and were told to challenge anyone who looked suspicious. My buddy and I decided to go to the flight line, check on our planes, and let our ground crews know what was going on. Our airfield was on the major highway between Liege and Brussels, and our planes were parked less than 50 yards from that road; a fence was in between. As we were checking our planes and talking to our crew chiefs, we heard the noise of armored vehicles, so we ran over to the road. Out of the fog came a British light-armored unit, and we hailed them down. Their commander stopped the whole outfit.

"Hey, Yank, can you tell us where we are?"

"You're on the road to Liege."

"But where? We're a bit lost."

"Well, if it'll help, you're 25 miles south of Brussels."

He studied his map for a few minutes and still seemed confused, so we marked our position for him.

"Well, jolly good. We've been sent to help out some Yanks up forward. Where are the Boche?"

Jim answered, "We don't know, but if you keep goin' down this road, you're bound to find 'em."

We were glad to see these guys.

"Do you need some cigarettes?" I asked. "Righto, old boy. Can you spare any?"

"Sure, take these." We gave them all we had.

"Well, must be off. Don't worry. We'll hold 'em off. Cheerio." And with a wave to us, he told his driver to get going, and they disappeared into the fog.

We felt a lot better now and told our crew chiefs things would probably be okay. We hung around the flight line for awhile, had lunch with our ground crews, which upset the engineering officer because it wasn't proper for officers to eat with the enlisted men, bummed some cigarettes, and were finally ready to go back to the ready-room when we heard the noise of half-tracks again; this time it was coming from the other direction. We ran out to the road, and sure enough, it was the same British outfit we had talked to a couple of hours earlier.

"What happened?" we asked.

"They've got heavy stuff up there, Tiger tanks. We're no match for them, so we're pulling back."

"Jesus Christ! You can't go back. We could lose all these planes."

He looked apologetic and said, "Sorry, Yank. Those are our orders. I think they're going to try to bring some other stuff in for you, but I'm not sure—anyway—good luck." And he headed off into the fog. I felt like asking for my cigarettes back. When the noise of the column had died away, we had a very lonely feeling. Could it really happen? Could we lose this airfield to the Germans?

Late in the afternoon there was an urgent meeting. We were told that a German paratroops unit was going to parachute in that night to capture the field; after all, it had been theirs, and they knew the area well. Supposedly some troops would be coming to defend the place, but nobody knew what troops or when they would arrive.

We had been getting very little direction from higher headquarters; it seemed it would be up to the various fighter-bomber group commanders to handle things the way they saw it. We were told some of the squadrons at other bases had already flown their planes out.

All our enlisted men had rifles, some the M-1 Garand and others the M-1 Carbine; the ground officers had carbines, and the pilots had 45 automatic pistols. This was hardly the arsenal needed to defeat a group of highly trained paratroopers, but that's all we had. I doubt if any man had spent more than a half a day on the rifle range, and they were not equipped mentally or physically to engage in combat. Be that as it may, the men were put in positions around the field and our compound.

By 2000 hours no troops had arrived to take over the defense of the field, so if the Germans attacked, it would be up to the cooks, the bakers, the mechanics, and the clerks, plus some very inexperienced ground officers and a bunch of pilots, to do the job.

Things were getting hairy. The pilots were out encouraging the enlisted men who were damn scared, as well they should be, and hoping no trigger-happy jerk would shoot them by mistake. One of the men asked Jim what he should do if he saw a German; he said he was so scared he couldn't think.

He told Jim, "Don't worry. Once the shooting starts you'll be okay. If you see someone floating down, aim at him and just pull the trigger."

The word was passed for the pilots to assemble in the ready-room. When we arrived, we were told that the German paratroopers were on their way, and the decision had been made to fly the planes out. We all objected.

"Holy shit! It's nine o'clock at night. You can't see more than 200 feet, and the weather's the same all over the continent. There's no God damn place to land."

**138**

# CHAPTER 26: BIG BATTLES

We were to stand by in the ready-room awaiting orders to head for our planes. The pilots who did not have planes would be moved out by truck; they were too valuable to be left behind in what would probably be a slaughter.

The next report came in. The planes carrying the paratroopers had hit our first line of antiaircraft guns and had been severely mauled. That was the first good news we'd had in over a week. A short time later came the next report. At our secondary line of antiaircraft defense over half of their planes had been shot down. They were no longer a viable attack force.

The tension was extreme—like a high voltage current waiting to discharge. Fortunately, we weren't drinking. Things were too serious to be faced half bombed, and we might have to be flying shortly, under the worst possible conditions. And finally good news. What was left of the paratrooper force had turned back. Thanks to our antiaircraft fire they had been rendered impotent and apparently chose to save what was left and go back home. We immediately got drunk.

The next day was a cliffhanger. First we were told that things had improved and our field was no longer in danger. Then two hours later we were called again to a meeting and told to stand by to evacuate the field. Clearly no one knew what the real situation was.

So now we were all in the ready-room waiting and talking over what we could do. Morgan, one of the flight leaders, addressed the squadron commander and said he had a plan; we eagerly listened. Even though Morgan was one of the old boys, he had been very nice to us and had our respect, not only as an excellent flight leader, but as a good guy as well.

"I've checked the weather, and even though it's lousy, it's better than it's been. We have at least a 200-foot ceiling, and you can see damn near to the end of the runway, at least a mile. I think we could take flights of two airplanes, fly on the deck, down the road, and find the German advance column. We've bombed from less than 200 feet plenty of times. I think we could knock them out."

His proposal received an immediate response.

"Hell, yes. Let's try it. It's better than sittin' on our ass doin' nothin'."

"I'm with you, Morgan. What about it, Major?" (The major was our squadron commander.)

He was not enthusiastic. "I can't authorize that. At the slowest speed you could fly, you'd cover that mile in 15 seconds or less. By the time you spotted anything, you'd be by him. I'm sorry, but the answer is no. I'm trying to get through this thing without losing any pilots or planes."

"But what about our airfield? We don't want to lose it," someone asked.

"We can always get another airfield," he answered.

Of course he was right, but we weren't happy with his decision. Morgan's plan was risky, but it did have a slight chance of success. We asked our infantry liaison officer if he could give us any plan at all or any idea what we should do.

"Yes, if they get close, get the hell outta here." We'd had better days. Early Christmas Eve morning we were awakened by a hell of a commotion. The operations clerk was coming down the hall, opening every door, turning on lights, and yelling, "All pilots report to the ready-room immediately." It could only mean one of two things; the Germans were just down the road, and we had to get out, or we could fly.

When we stepped outside our quarters, we had the answer; even though it was still dark, we could see the stars.

Briefing was simple and direct; we were to head for the battle area and start killing Germans. We grabbed some breakfast, made a fast trip to the can, and were off the ground by first light, and we weren't alone. Every fighter-bomber group in the Ninth Air Force was heading for the Battle of the Bulge. Some of the Luftwaffe squadrons had finally decided to join the fight, and things got real exciting.

The next day—Christmas Day—the battle continued. Our control center (J.O.C.) came under attack and asked for help. We were only a few miles away so told them we'd be there momentarily. A P-51 outfit also heard the call on a different frequency and also told the controller they'd be there in a couple of minutes. We were flying east; the P-51s were flying west. Both of us were above a partial cloud cover, and both of us broke through it at the same time over the control center.

As I broke through the clouds, I saw 8 to 10 fighters breaking through and on a diving pattern toward the J.O.C.

The P-51 pilots saw the same thing from their position. The P-51 and the Me 109 are quite similar in appearance from that angle. The P-47 is quite similar in appearance to an FW 190 from that angle.

We closed for a fight but fortunately recognized each other before the shooting started, and nowhere did we see any German fighters. We called the J.O.C. and asked where they were, and the controller said in a rather panicked voice, "They're right over the top of us. We need help."

Our squadron leader answered, "Are they shooting at you?"

"No," came the reply.

The squadron leader then said, "They're not shooting at you because they're gone. We're right over you now, and there's some P-51s with us." So somehow in the excitement of things either the Germans got away or maybe they never were there.

We continued on toward the Bastone area, and the sky was getting damn full of airplanes. The battle area was quite small compared to the number of fighter-bomber groups that were occupying that airspace. It wasn't exactly a traffic jam, but you could always see Thunderbolts wherever you looked.

For the first couple of days we didn't have a front line ground controller, but we didn't need one; the Germans were everywhere. We had been ordered to go after the tanks and armored vehicles, and we found plenty of them. The only problem was there were so many targets that we ran out of ammunition in a hurry, which meant at least a one-and-a-half or two hour turn-around time before we could get back to the target area.

For the next week we flew mission after mission to the Bulge, but it was no longer a Bulge, just a blip on the map. After four days Germans were getting hard to find, but we discovered something on an early morning mission that explained it; they were hiding in the forests.

A pilot reported he saw tracks going into a small wooded area but none coming out the other side. Obviously the tanks were still in the woods hiding from the fighter-bombers. Another pilot reported seeing clouds of exhaust smoke coming out of a small forested area; there was no village there, so it had to be German armored vehicles. Our intelligence reports coming from the front were telling us the Germans were still there in force. So it was now a simple matter of figuring out what was happening. The Germans were bringing their armored vehicles and tanks out at night, but at dawn they retreated to the woods to hide themselves from us. We started bombing and strafing the woods, and sure enough that's where they were.

By New Year's Day there was no more Battle of the Bulge as far as the fighter-bombers were concerned. The German attack had been halted, and now our ground forces were in the initial stages of regrouping, reinforcing, and preparing to take back the ground they had lost. Bastogne had been liberated, General Patton was getting in high gear, and the weather was holding clear. By the end of the second week of January the Battle of the Bulge was officially over, and our ground forces were pushing east into Germany.

Official battle histories are always written from a certain perspective. The army wants to make the army look good. The same applies to the air force, marines, navy, and coast guard. There have been many books written about the Battle of the Bulge. General Patton, in his book *War As I Knew It*, devotes more pages to it than to any other battle in the European campaign. Hollywood even made a movie or two about the Battle of the Bulge.

I find it interesting to note that General Patton, although a staunch supporter of the Fighter-Bomber Boys, concluded that the victory was due to his battlefield wisdom and superior fighting ability. The general was a great man, but he was just too proud to admit that his superior battlefield wisdom and fighting ability were impotent without the Fighter-Bomber Boys. Facts are facts. The Germans attacked en masse only once and that was on December 19. That was the first day the Thunderbolts were grounded due to weather. The Germans advanced through American lines, got into Belgium, and were ready for a dash to the sea. Our forces were beaten back at every turn except for those gallant bastards of Bastogne; that was the only American position that held. Now, what occurred that allowed this to happen? The answer is that the Thunderbolt fighter-bombers were grounded due to weather. And if the American troops were being beaten back, and they were, what suddenly changed that allowed them to stop the German advance and go on the offensive again? The answer is that the Thunderbolt fighter-bombers were finally able to get off the ground and go to work. There is absolutely no question that they were the weapon that changed that battle from defeat to victory.

In the other two deciding battles of the war, the Normandy invasion and the Breakout at Saint-Lo, the Thunderbolts played an important role, but they were only one part of a massive military force. In the Battle of the Bulge they were the single force that broke the back of the German army. It proved beyond question that when the Fighter-Bomber Boys were out of action, our ground forces, as heroic as they were, were so evenly matched with the German army that the battle could go either way. Our forces, geared to the attack, were not a defensive power, and therefore, lost ground under the German onslaught when the air arm was denied them.

# chapter 27

# THE BIRDS ARE WALKING

No story about the life of the Fighter-Bomber Boys would be complete without relating the flying conditions they had to cope with because of weather. During training if the weather was bad we didn't fly, but combat operations were entirely different. As I've said before, while flying from England, all our missions were group missions. That meant three squadrons of three flights each, and sometimes, for especially important targets, a fourth flight was added to each squadron; that would be a total of 48 planes rather than the usual 36. It took about 15 minutes to get those planes off the ground and assembled in formation and ready to head for the target. It was no problem as long as the weather was clear, but how do you handle it with a ceiling of 300 feet and visibility less than a mile?

It would be a cinch for one plane to take off and climb through the overcast, but what about 48 planes? Well, it was possible, and here's how we did it. The group leader (also leader of the first squadron) took off, climbed to just under the overcast, and started a wide circle to the left. The rest of that squadron followed at 15-second intervals, each plane shortening the circle until all planes in the squadron linked up in formation. Then the group leader set course for the target and started up through the overcast on instruments. The flight to his right made a 2-degree turn to the right, flew that heading for 1 minute, then turned to the same heading as the group leader. The flight on his left made their 2-degree turn to the left, flew that heading for a minute, then took up the same heading as the group leader. The other squadrons took off, assembled, and followed the same procedure and started up through the overcast.

Only the flight leader flew on instruments; the other members of his flight tucked in close and flew formation on him. Number four man had the toughest position because he was flying formation on the element leader who was flying formation on the flight leader; number four was on the end of a whipsaw.

When I say close formation, I mean CLOSE. In order to see you had to have your wing tucked in between your leader's wing tip and fuselage; if the planes were parked that close together on the ground, you could jump from plane to plane. This type of flying required absolute concentration, great skill, and a high proficiency in instrument flying. But there was one problem: fighter pilots historically were lousy instrument pilots. Instrument flying was not a priority in the early days of training fighter pilots. But the air war in Europe changed that. When the 8th Fighter Command started operations in Europe, their mission was to escort bombers, and they had to fly in all kinds of weather. Their lack of instrument training could, and did, impair that mission. To remedy this shortcoming, replacement fighter pilots were given increased instrument training, both in cadet school and at their replacement training squadrons. The result was that the replacement pilots were much more proficient than the old boys, but the old boys were the flight leaders. It would have been much better to let a replacement pilot lead the flight through the overcast, but this was obviously unthinkable under the old boy system.

Under these circumstances there were bound to be accidents, and there were. If the flight got split apart, each pilot had to immediately go on instruments on his own and hope no one else was in his airspace. There were midair collisions. It happened twice in my squadron, but fortunately the pilots either bailed out or made an emergency landing.

Once we arrived in France (July 1944) weather ceased to be a problem for several months, but by September we again faced horrible flying conditions. The war was still going on, and we continued to fly, but on many days flying was impossible. We had a triple problem; we needed reasonably good weather at our field and good weather at the target, so we could see what we were hitting, and then the weather had to be good enough when we returned to base so that we could land without smashing up all of our aircraft. I'm sure that many a ground soldier who desperately needed our support at the front, where the weather was good, was told that he'd get no air support because of bad weather. But to him the weather was okay, so— "where are those fucking fly boys—probably chasing pussy at their officers' club." Unfortunately for him the weather at our base was socked in, and we were grounded. Unfortunately for us there was nothing to chase and no officers' club. We were living in the mud just as he was, but we always realized that no matter how bad it was for us—it was worse for him.

The British had excellent radar, much better than ours, and they'd been at this business of war far longer than we. Losing planes to combat operations was just part of war; losses were to be expected. But to lose aircraft and crews because of weather was a sorry situation, and the Brits did something about it. I've said that war brings out the very worst and the very best in those who participate in it. Sometimes impossible problems were solved by far-out ideas. One such example was how to land airplanes in zero-zero weather. At that time radar had not progressed to the point of guiding a pilot to a landing in zero-zero weather; that feat was not accomplished until 1945 after the war in Europe had ended. But the fact that the technology did not exist at that time didn't stop the British; they simply invented a different technology.

They had an airfield with an extremely long runway that was used for emergency landings. So they dug up both sides of that runway and laid in pipes with nozzles about every 20 feet. Gasoline was fed to these nozzles, and when the weather was socked in all over England, they would simply turn on the gas and light each nozzle; the heat generated was so intense it dissipated the fog over the field so planes could see to land. It was ingenious, and it worked. It's interesting to note that a similar system was installed at the Los Angeles International Airport in the late 1940s or early 1950s. There was lots of publicity about it and a demonstration given on a foggy day. The mayor boasted that Los Angeles had the only all-weather airport in the world. If memory serves me correctly it was called F.I.D.O. Well, after all the back-slapping was over, the system died a quiet death, for it was never used. It was just too damn dangerous for commercial flying.

By November 1944, we were facing very dangerous weather conditions. We might take off on a mission in fairly decent weather only to find the field socked in when we returned. Some of these landings were so hairy that you thought about hanging up your parachute and never flying again, but naturally you didn't.

There was a major battle called "Operation Queen" scheduled for November 12, 1944. It was the kickoff for our advance into Germany. At that time, largely due to weather, the front was at a stalemate. The weather on the 12th was worse than no good, and the same followed for the 13th and the 14th. We had been on alert since the 11th, so naturally we were a little uptight. The battle couldn't be launched without the Thunderbolt fighter-bombers, so everything was on hold. Finally it was predicted that the weather would clear on the 16th, so the battle was launched early that day. The weather did clear at the front but not in the rear areas where the airfields were.

We were told to fly the mission anyway even though we may have nowhere to land when we returned. So we took off on instruments, individually, and climbed through the overcast, which was only a few thousand feet. This was such a big battle that we flew a group mission—one of the very few we flew after leaving England. Every fighter-bomber group in that area participated, and there were Thunderbolts all over the sky. It was one hell of a battle. The ceiling at the front was about 2,000 feet, and there were about three groups of us along a 3-mile front.

The artillery barrage ceased as we arrived, which was standard procedure. We didn't want our own artillery shells flying through the same airspace that we were using. The colored panels were out marking our side of the front. We were working within 50 to 100 yards of those panels, so the ground guys had a ring-side seat.

In this battle we were at a distinct disadvantage. We had to stay under 2,000 feet because of the overcast, so we were always within range of those deadly German quadmount 20-millimeter flak guns, and those guys knew how to use them. They were also backed up by plenty of 88s and 155s. There were explosions all over the place. Bombs were going off and fires raging on the ground; the air was thick with flak; Thunderbolts were diving, bombing, strafing, climbing, and turning. Some were hit, on fire, and on their way into the ground; some exploded in midair. It was one son of a bitch of a battle. When we were ready to leave, the groups were all separated. I had my flight with me but couldn't find the rest of my squadron. The radio was a constant jabber, calls for help, calls for location and direction, and pathetic calls, "I'm hit; I'm going in," and "Bail out; you're on fire." The pilots who participated in that battle on the morning of November 16, 1944, will remember it forever.

We ran into weather shortly after leaving the target and had to climb up above the overcast. As we neared our field, I was told it was socked in and given a heading to another field. When I arrived there, it was socked in, and I was told there was no place to land. I headed back to our field. We were flying at 10,000 feet, which put us about 2,000 feet over the top of the clouds. I knew I should be close to home, but how close? Suddenly a hole opened up, and directly below was an airfield. I told my flight we'd dive straight through that hole, and we did. We pulled out over the field at about 500 feet and going over 400 miles per hour just as the hole closed. I chopped everything back, bled off the excess speed, and landed. Wow! What a break! It was our own airfield. We were back home in one piece. Only seven planes from my squadron returned from that mission, but we only lost one pilot who must have been shot down at the target. The other four crash-landed somewhere between the front and our base, and by late the next day the four had all returned. That was the second time I had the distinct feeling that I was expendable.

Someone very high in command had to make the decision to launch the fighter-bombers, knowing that many might be lost due to weather alone; the alternative was to cancel the attack. Think of the responsibility that man had on his shoulders. I imagine it was Eisenhower himself. I don't think General Bradley would have made it on his own without Eisenhower's knowledge and approval. But then that's what generals are supposed to do; they make the tough decisions and have to live with the results. The men who do battle based on those decisions are the ones who die from it. But, as I've said before, war and death are inseparable. Decisions have to be made, battles have to be fought, and men have to die. Every pilot who flew a combat mission knew full well that he could die that day, maybe as soon as a half hour after takeoff. Why did he do it? Because his country needed him; it was that simple.

Shortly after this fiasco our own people came up with a solution to landing in bad weather. It wasn't as elaborate as the emergency field in England, but they used the same technology albeit on a very primitive level. They placed 55-gallon drums of gasoline about every 30 feet along both sides of the runway and lighted them. That generated enough heat to lift the fog to about 300 feet, and it also caused a very distinct red glow in the fog. So you looked for the glow, headed toward it while still on instruments, and soon you saw a tunnel of fire with a runway at the bottom. Our lack of accurate radar was overcome by having our own anti-aircraft guns fire so their shells would converge directly over our runway. If the top of the overcast was 10,000 feet, we'd fly at 14,000 and ask for a burst at 11,000. All eyes scanned the sky, and sure enough, there were the big black smudges just over the tops of the clouds. We immediately set up a heading using the smudge as a reference point and made a steep decline, on instruments, through the overcast. We went one flight at a time, each plane in trail.

This was true Yankee ingenuity, unsophisticated, simple, basic, and yes, crude, but it worked. In spite of the horrible landing conditions because of weather, we never had a landing accident. It was just too damn dangerous, and you couldn't afford to screw up, but after a landing under those conditions, it was great to be back on the ground in one piece.

# chapter 28

# ATTITUDE

We were used to winning. That attitude developed in the very beginning when the Thunderbolt groups were flying from England. There was an abundance of targets, and most were not too heavily defended, so the groups and squadrons got in the habit of always hitting their target and being victorious in battle. Consequently a mystique developed: the Fighter-Bomber Boys in their P-47 Thunderbolts were invincible. Weather alone, not the enemy, was the only thing that could prevent a successful mission.

Once ground support operations began after D-Day, the Luftwaffe would put in an appearance, appear to start an engagement—just enough to cause the Thunderbolts to jettison their bombs and prepare for air-to-air combat—then break off and retreat. This meant there would be no bombs to support the ground troops who were desperately waiting for help. Naturally the Thunderbolt pilots felt it was much more important to engage enemy fighters than enemy ground troops; after all, they were primarily fighter pilots. This serious breach of combat procedure was very quickly stopped. They were ordered—not advised, but ordered—to disregard the Luftwaffe and proceed to the assigned target in all cases. They could only jettison bombs and engage in a dogfight if they were attacked first. Just to make sure this order was faithfully carried out, the threat of courts martial was added. The final word was given to the pilots this way, "If you jettison your bombs to engage the Luftwaffe, you'd better have some holes in your airplane when you come home. This is the only acceptable proof that you were attacked first."

How did the Fighter-Bomber Boys react to this? Just as one would expect. They didn't like it, but they followed orders.

Once we gave up the U.S. Navy system of dive-bombing and began to develop our own technique, our accuracy increased dramatically. Each pilot wanted to be known as the best hitter in the squadron. Flak, no matter how intense, would not prevent that pilot from closing with his assigned target and destroying it. The navy system of releasing bombs from 3,000 feet was probably good enough to hit an aircraft carrier a city block long, but it was totally worthless when going after a heavy artillery piece dug in in a gun pit 20 feet in diameter or a tank eight feet wide. In order to hit that kind of target you had to release within the length of a football field, and that's exactly what we did.

The winning attitude prevailed. By now, having our own pilots as air-ground controllers, our high degree of accuracy in bombing, and the fact that no group or squadron of Thunderbolt fighter-bombers had ever been defeated in battle was a real morale booster. We were damn good, and we knew it. There was, however, a day of reckoning coming.

I've mentioned that during the Battle of the Bulge we were told we may have to evacuate our field as the German offensive ground on. Fortunately we did not have to, but another Thunderbolt group closer to the German spearhead than we were did. It was the 368th Fighter Group, and their airfield was at Chievres, Belgium. Actually they had been scheduled to move anyway because the tactical air commands were being realigned, but the Battle of the Bulge speeded up the time table.

They left their field on December 26, 1944, and went to Rheims, France. This was probably just an interim location because there were two other groups operating from there. But no one anticipated what was to occur a few days later.

On January 1, 1945, at about 9:30 A.M., a large force of German ME 109s attacked the 365th Fighter Group based at Metz, France. Within 10 minutes the German pilots had destroyed 32 P-47 Thunderbolts, all on the ground. About half of the attacking German aircraft were shot down, but that did not lessen the fact that the Thunderbolt fighter-bomber group had been put out of action at a very critical point in the war. Fortunately, one of their squadrons had taken off on a ground support mission a short time before the Luftwaffe attacked; even so, the group was effectively out of action. However, help was on the way.

The 368th Fighter Group, temporarily at Rheims, was immediately sent to Metz, and as one of their pilots told me, "As I was landing at what was to be our new field, Thunderbolts that had been bombed and strafed by the ME 109s that morning were still burning."

That battle was indeed a victory for the Luftwaffe but not a defeat for the Fighter-Bomber Boys. No pilots had been killed, and the aircraft were quickly replaced. The 365th was back in business in a short time—back to supporting our front line troops and killing Germans. This incident brought home the fact that even though Germany was now beaten and had definitely lost the war, they were still a formidable enemy and capable of successful combat operations. Even though those German pilots had badly mauled one of our groups, they had our respect. Attacking enemy airfields was without question the toughest target of all, and the pilots engaged in those missions could always expect heavy losses. The attack did not affect our winning attitude. It had not been an air-to-air battle; except for antiaircraft fire, the Luftwaffe had been unopposed. Actually it made us even more self-confident than ever to know firsthand just how devastating a bombing and strafing attack could be. We were still the victors, the winged warriors. Every day brought us closer to final victory, but it was still many months away.

# chapter 29

# THE CREW CHIEF

Late model Thunderbolts were coming off the assembly line, and by October we were receiving more than enough to replace our losses. I was now the squadron test pilot. I replaced the guy who had done the job from the beginning. He was an excellent pilot, and after flying well over 60 missions and collecting a Purple Heart, was being sent home. A test involved putting the plane through every violent maneuver it would be expected to encounter on a combat mission. It was dangerous but exciting. One day two new planes arrived, and the squadron commander told me to test both of them and pick one for myself; he'd take the other. The new models were greatly improved with a full bubble canopy for better visibility, bigger gas tanks for longer range, more power, and supposedly, better maneuverability. Both planes tested perfectly, and I couldn't decide which one I wanted. Then I wondered what would happen to his old plane. I had flown it several times and considered it the best Thunderbolt I'd ever been in. Also, it had been lucky for me. I'd never been hit in that airplane. Regardless of the new models, I decided I wanted it. When I reported back, I delivered a broad hint.

"Sir, both of the new planes are okay. I really couldn't detect any difference in them."

"Which one do you want?"

"Well, Major, I was wondering what you are going to do with your old plane."

"It'll be assigned to the next pilot up for his own plane," he answered.

"Sir, I'd rather have your plane."

"But the new ones are better."

"I know, sir, but I have a special feeling for your plane. I've never picked up a piece of flak in it. It's lucky for me."

"I know. That's why you're the only one I'll let fly it—if I'm not flying it myself. Tell you what. If you want it, it's yours, but you'll have to take my crew chief with it. He's a good crew chief, but he's always in trouble, and it's an embarrassment to me."

I couldn't believe my luck; not only was I getting the plane I wanted but the best crew chief in the squadron. True, he couldn't stay out of trouble. His last escapade was to get drunk, steal the engineering officer's jeep, and wreck it; it cost him his stripes. But that didn't diminish his love for that airplane.

"Thanks, Major. I'll try and straighten him out, but I'm not promising anything. . . ."

"With his record I'm not expecting anything."

I saluted and left his office.

This squadron commander had replaced our previous one—the one with the personality problem—and this guy was good. He was an excellent leader, both in the air and on the ground, a superb pilot, gutsy and aggressive in combat, and just one hell of a fine man.

Later in the day I told Jim about my new plane and crew chief, got a fifth of whiskey out of my private stock, and said I was going to the flight line; he tagged along but hung around his plane, out of earshot, when I talked to my new crew chief.

"Chief," I began, "this is my airplane now, and you're my crew chief. Here's some whiskey to celebrate."

He was all smiles as I gave him the bottle.

"Now, listen. I've got something to tell you. The old man got rid of you cuz you're a screw-up; he gave me his plane only on the condition I take you with it. You could be crewing his new plane."

"I'd rather stay with this one, sir."

"I know you're a good crew chief, probably the best in the squadron, but why can't you stay out of trouble?"

He hung his head, gave me his little-boy-in-trouble expression, and said, "I don't know, Lieutenant; it just seems to happen."

"Well, I want you to knock that crap off. I'm giving you this booze. You can get quietly drunk in your tent tonight, but if you get in trouble, I'll never give you a drop again—got that?"

"Yes, sir."

"And I'll ride your ass into the ground. You got that too?"

"Yes, sir."

I put my hand out and we shook. "Chief, you keep that baby in good shape, and maybe we'll both stick around for awhile." As I was leaving I turned and said, "Stay out of trouble, and I'll get your stripes back." He just smiled.

I've already mentioned the relationship between the pilot and his crew chief. It was unique, truly something special.

My job as the test pilot was not only to check out new planes but planes that had been shot up and repaired. Once repairs were completed, the engineering officer, who was in charge of the flight line, had to certify the plane fit for combat. On a couple of occasions those planes did not perform satisfactorily. It finally came to a head when a plane I was testing had a flap malfunction on landing. One flap came down, but the other one jammed causing the plane to go into a roll. I barely recovered before hitting the ground. Upon investigation I found that the entire right wing of that plane had been replaced with a wing from an older model, and the hydraulic systems were not compatible. He knew it but certified the plane anyway.

We had a hell of an argument over this. I was a first lieutenant. He was a captain and felt, because he outranked me, he would prevail. But the pilot always has the final say-so as to the airworthiness of an aircraft, especially the squadron test pilot. I wanted him relieved of duty, but the squadron commander settled it. The captain had to make a public apology at the pilots' daily meeting and promise to pay closer personal attention to maintenance and repairs in the future. I dropped my complaint, but I had made an enemy.

A short time later my crew chief was put on K.P. Obviously this was the engineering officer's method of getting back at me. I decided to have a showdown with him. His office was in the main repair hangar, and I found him gloating behind his desk.

"My crew chief is on K.P. Crew chiefs don't do K.P. I want him off right now."

"Lieutenant, your crew chief is a private, and privates do K.P. He stays, and I'm sir to you." Just the two of us were in the room. I kept my voice low so I wouldn't be overheard, leaned over his desk, and poked my finger in his face.

"I'll give you 30 seconds to get him off K.P., or I'll break your fuckin' neck."

He blanched, hesitated a moment, and said with a shaky voice, "I don't care if he's on K.P. or not. I'll take him off."

"Now!" I said. "And another thing—don't ever mess with my crew chief again. You got a problem with him, you come to me."

"But he's under my control."

"Not my crew chief." And with that I left. I never had trouble with that guy again.

Why am I relating this story? Because it happened, and it illustrates the human side of things. His job was to get aircraft back into service as fast as possible, and he was willing to overlook a few things that he considered minor problems just to make his record look good. But there are no minor problems once you leave the ground. Engine failure over enemy territory means either death, or, if you're lucky, a POW camp for the rest of the war.

It also shows conflicts were bound to occur between the support people and ourselves. They worked every day in all kinds of weather and got very little thanks for it. So it was necessary, occasionally, to clearly define our respective roles. We had one job to do; they had another—and as I've said before, everyone didn't love everyone else. Living in such unnatural conditions, that's understandable, but the military order of things always kept that powder keg from exploding.

# chapter 30
# GOING HOME

**B**y early November we were very low on pilots, but the end of November brought the largest group of replacements we'd ever received. Some of them flew their first missions during the Battle of the Bulge.

In mid-January I was told I was going home. I flew my last mission and thought what a cruel twist of fate it would be if I was killed now. But the God of War smiled, and as I returned from the mission and touched down on the runway, I wondered if I'd ever fly the beloved Thunderbolt again.

After I was out of the cockpit, having a cigarette with my crew chief, I told him I'd be leaving, and he was visibly moved. Later in the day I brought him a fifth of whiskey and thanked him for helping me stay alive. By now he had three of his stripes back. There was a stack of 1,000-pound bombs near my plane, so we sat on them, and he looked hesitantly at me and said, "Can we have a drink together, Lieutenant?" Of course this was strictly against the rules, but so what.

"Damn right, Chief. I'd be proud to drink with you but watch out for your boss" (the engineering officer). "He's not my boss, sir; you are."

We sipped from the bottle. Soon it was time for me to go.

"Chief, I'll miss you. You're the best crew chief any pilot could have. Take care of yourself—and thanks."

My butt was cold from sitting on those bombs. The weather had turned and clouds were forming. We slid to the ground, stood up, and shook hands.

"Lieutenant," he hesitated and hung his head, which was his habit when he had something to say, "you're the best pilot I've ever had—the only one who ever gave a shit about me. I wish you were stayin', but I'm glad you're leavin'."

I got in the jeep and drove away.

That night we had a party of sorts. We all would receive packages from home occasionally but would save the goodies for special occasions; this was a special occasion. Jim was scheduled to leave in a couple of weeks. Actually he should have gone first because he had flown more missions than I had, but I'd ruptured my ears a couple of times, and they weren't healing. Each dive-bombing attack made them worse, so the flight surgeon told me I was going to a hospital for treatment before I returned to the States.

"How long you gonna be in the hospital?" Jim asked.

"Don't know. Doc said a couple of weeks maybe."

"Shit, you lucky bastard. I wish I was going with you."

"So do I."

We drank our booze, and I continued to pack.

"Jim," I began, "what are you gonna do after the war?"

"I don't know, but I want to be a civilian, probably go back to school—if I make it through the next two weeks."

"You'll make it—just play it cool. Don't try to be a hero."

"Naw. I'm through with that crap. I just want to finish up and go home."

We got very drunk that night. Other guys dropped in to say good-bye, and in the morning, when I said my final good-bye to them, it was a difficult parting. I had a lump in my throat as big as an elephant turd.

Within a month the Fighter-Bomber Boys were flying from fields in Germany. The Luftwaffe was so depleted that it was no longer an effective force against the bombers, and they began putting in an appearance at the front. The fighter-bomber pilots finally got a chance at air-to-air combat, but encounters were rare.

Experienced fighter pilots knew if things went wrong they could always break off and still have enemy planes to fight tomorrow. Our guys were so eager for a dogfight, feeling it might be their only chance, they often used poor judgment. A friend of mine in another squadron was in a flight of four Thunderbolts, and they were lucky enough to encounter some ME 109s. My friend got on the tail of one and chased him in and out of some clouds, finally closing and getting in some good hits. He knew another ME 109 was on his tail, but he wouldn't let go of his prey. He told me he wasn't going to miss his kill. Well, he shot the guy down, but the German fighter on his tail set him on fire. He bailed out but was badly burned. Unfortunately, he was over enemy territory and was captured. Even though civilians captured him, they treated him well and got him to a hospital where he spent the next two and a half months until the war was over. Unfortunately there was no witness to his victory and obviously his gun camera film was destroyed with his plane, so he never got credit for shooting down that German fighter that cost him so dearly.

# CHAPTER 30: GOING HOME

Another example of the fanatical desire to find and fight the Luftwaffe was demonstrated by a radio conversation overheard one day. Apparently a flight had been on alert, parked at the takeoff end of the runway, and were scrambled by the controller to intercept enemy fighters. Once the lead pilot was in the air he checked in.

"Scramble Control, this is Scramble Leader. I'm airborne with bases loaded."

This meant he had four planes including himself.

"Roger, Scramble Leader. Head one-four-zero. We have a flight of 12 bandits at 10,000 feet, approximately eight miles."

"Roger, Scramble Control. We're on our way."

"Scramble Flight from Scramble Leader. We're going to war emergency power."

War emergency power was a system of water injection and additional fuel that increased the engine horsepower by 15 percent. After his instructions to his flight, there was a short pause and then:

"Scramble Leader from Scramble two. There are only four of us."

"Roger, Scramble two. Makes the odds in our favor. Don't feel sorry for 'em."

Unfortunately the bandits turned out to be friendlies, so in frustration the scramble flight returned to base.

The death knell for the Luftwaffe was administered in late March and early April when several groups of P-47 Thunderbolts attacked the remaining German air bases and destroyed their planes on the ground. These were exceptionally tough missions because air fields were always heavily defended. But true to their tradition, the Fighter-Bomber Boys bombed and strafed them into oblivion, and the Luftwaffe ceased to be a fighting force.

By now the German army was disintegrating, and troops were surrendering en masse and, as all things must come to an end, so did the war in Europe. Bombs no longer were slung under the wings of the Thunderbolts, and plugs covered the machine gun barrels; they would no longer shoot in anger. The Fighter-Bomber Boys had done their job, earned their money, and paid their dues. The fighting and killing was over. It was now time to go home. But you would never be a young man again even though you were barely in your twenties.

## chapter 31

# HOMECOMING

It was not as joyous as I expected. I felt guilty because I left the squadron while the war was still going on. They were still fighting. I was safely home. I felt guilty about being alive. Why me? Why did I survive when so many of my friends had been killed? My parents didn't know quite how to act. When my mother looked at me, I could see pity and compassion, but I rejected it. I just could not respond.

Gasoline was rationed, but because I was home on leave from overseas, I was eligible for gas stamps, so I went to the ration board to get them. I presented my leave orders and was given enough for 12 gallons. I asked for more but was told that was all I was entitled to. I thought of my Thunderbolt using 100 gallons an hour—how ironic. In a controlled rage I threw the ration book back at the clerk, cursed the whole ration board out, and headed for the door, but was stopped by an older woman. She took me to her office and gave me enough stamps for 100 gallons and said to come back if I needed more. So, there were people who cared, people who tried to understand.

A few nights later I was driving to one of the bars our gang used to frequent when an old man stepped off the curb right in front of me, and I hit him. Someone called the police and an ambulance and, of course, I had to wait at the scene. I walked over and looked at the guy lying in the street, saw his blood on the pavement, and felt only anger toward him for causing me this delay, no sympathy, no compassion, only anger. My God! What had happened to me? And then I knew: The person I used to be no longer exists. The person I am now is who I am. In order to survive I made myself invulnerable to emotion. Now I must relearn what it's like to feel compassion, forgiveness, love, but based on how I felt, that wouldn't be easy.

There was a surprising number of the old gang around, but it wasn't the same. None of them had seen combat duty. At this point we didn't have a hell of a lot in common. When my leave was up, I reported to the Miramar Hotel in Santa Monica. The air corps had taken it over as a reception and reassignment center for returning pilots. I had not felt comfortable while home on leave, but the minute I walked into the Miramar everything was fine. I was back among my peers. The majority were bomber pilots, B-17s and B-24s, with a few P-51 guys. I was the only Thunderbolt pilot. But we had all witnessed death in the air, had experienced the horror of German flak, had seen our closest friends die, and shared the relief of making it back alive. We understood each other.

But the wounds of war were too deep, the scars too permanent to simply go away. Soon after I became a civilian, they began to fester. It was a good dream; there I was with my old flying buddies, but they had been dead such a long time. It was a bad dream; the flak was all around me, but the airplane wouldn't move. I pushed the controls, but it made no difference. Christ! I'm going in, and then I was awake, sweating and my heart pounding like a trip-hammer. God damn it. Will this never stop?

But over the years it does go away, all except a few incidents that for some reason won't. They were no different than other strafing runs, yet, for some reason they are indelible.

We were attacking a railroad marshaling yard, and there were trains all over the place. I spotted one that was moving, which seemed strange because all the others were stopped. I made a tight turn and came in on the locomotive. I could see the engineer in the cab. Just before I began to shoot, things went into slow motion. I saw him pull a lanyard, and a puff of steam came out; he was blowing the train whistle. Why didn't he get out of there? He kept looking right at me, never looked away, and the train was still moving. I began to fire, and a split second later the locomotive exploded. What was he thinking at his instant of death? I often wish I had not squeezed the trigger. I can still see every detail, the locomotive, the puff of steam from the whistle—and him—looking right at me. That face has haunted me ever since.

Yes, we had a reason to kill: it was war. But turning middle-class teenagers into killers is one thing; returning them to their normal place in a postwar society is quite another matter.

At a recent reunion of my squadron some of us were talking about this subject. One of the guys said, "You know we did a lot of strafing—killed a lot of people (I noted he said people, not Germans), but there's one son of a bitch I can't get out of my mind. He was on a motorcycle, and I caught him with a full blast. Part of him stayed with the cycle, but most of him lit in the trees by the side of the road. You'd think after all these years that would go away," he looked down and shook his head subconsciously trying to cast out the image, "but it doesn't."

The rest of us understood. We were still fighting our own devils. Finally someone said, "It's seared into your brain. It won't go away until you're dead." We all silently agreed.

"Maybe not even then," I added, "but somehow we'll figure out how to handle it." That was the life of the Fighter-Bomber Boys.

# EPILOGUE

Was it worth it, the death, the sacrifice? Of course it was. Had we lost, Americans would have been slaves to the Japanese and the Germans; America would cease to exist. Did we learn anything? No! In five years we would be at war in Korea, and a small percentage of our youth would again be asked to die on foreign soil. At the end of World War II we were the most powerful nation on earth, but the Russian Bear was allowed, even helped, to become a rival dominant power totally opposed to our way of life and the principles so many of us had fought for and some had died for. Not a decade passed that did not see another call to arms. It was always the same story, our presidents proclaiming that America's vital interests were in jeopardy. So again and again our youths were sent. But the patriotic fervor was lacking. They were not fighting for their country or their family; they were fighting because the politicians had decided war was preferable to peace, and again our youth paid the price but did not reap the rewards.

World War II was the last honorable war. Where, if a man had to die, he knew what he was dying for. From then until now, wars involving the United States have simply been human sacrifice dictated by political or economic expediency. Those to be sacrificed may have volunteered or been chosen by lottery, and as they died in rice paddies and cockpits, I'm sure their final thought was—"God damn it; it wasn't worth it."

The military has always, and must always, remain under the control of the civil branch of government. But our wars since World War II have shown that some restrictions must be imposed on this practice. During the Korean War, President Truman ordered ammunition rationing for front line troops. It wasn't that we didn't have the ammunition to shoot, but we were not allowed to shoot more than one round a day from any heavy mortar, artillery piece, or rocket launcher. He forbade any attacks beyond the 38th parallel and constantly meddled in the field management of the war. As a result there was no victory.

In the Vietnam War, Lyndon Johnson decided which targets would be bombed and which would not. He decided how many troops were needed and how they'd be deployed. While he was actually planning a massive buildup of troops, he stood in front of national television and said, "American boys are not going to do what Asian boys should do," promising the fighting would be done by their young men not ours.

But his lies were nothing compared to Richard Nixon's. He promised while cam-

156

paigning that he had a plan to end the war; he was elected by a landslide. But he had no plan except to escalate the war. He denied to the American people that we were fighting in Cambodia when we were already suffering casualties there. Years later, after thousands of additional casualties, he finally surrendered but announced it as a victory, as the North Vietnamese took over the entire country—some victory.

Our latest charade in the Gulf continued this presidential tradition. George Bush, after spending months assembling a mighty military force to conquer a pip-squeak despot, finally unleashed it. But in 100 hours he said STOP. The result is that the despot continued on in power, and again we retired from the field of battle without a victory.

Politicians are quite adept at creating a situation where war seems the only solution. It is also interesting to note that wars consume gigantic amounts of ammunition and supplies of all kinds, especially expensive aircraft, armor, and ships, many of which are inevitably destroyed. These items must be replaced, and this stimulates the economy. Of course, the fact that this stimulation is all accomplished with borrowed money is never mentioned. The politicians can boast of full employment and take credit for good economic times. But the young men, and now women, who have to do the fighting never share in this prosperity; their reward is the fear, personal sacrifice, family disruption, and severe economic hardship. If they're lucky, they survive; if not, they become the human sacrifice. Is this what America stands for?

Our constitution gives the authority to declare war only to the Congress, but no Congress has been willing to accept that responsibility since 1941, yet tens of thousands of our youth have died on the field of battle since the end of World War II.

But there is a simple way to eliminate war. Other than World War II our wars have largely been due to economic stagnation and the powerful influence of our military industrial complex. If we take the profit out of war, war will cease to be attractive to corporate America. If we commit troops to combat, the entire country must bear the burden. That would mean no profits for anybody and everyone would be on the same pay scale as our soldiers in the field. Obviously this would be unacceptable to the American people, so our participation in future wars would also be unacceptable.

As we move toward the twenty-first century we must realize that war is an enterprise that can no longer be tolerated. The only worthwhile memorial to those who have fought and died in previous wars is to abolish war. We only have one life that we are aware of. It is our most precious possession; we cannot squander it to the God of War.

We have been around for a few million years. We have made great strides in medicine, transportation, the arts, communications, and other human endeavors. However, in no other field have we shown the propensity for supreme achievement that we have in the development of weapons to kill fellow human beings. In fact, we have reached the zenith by developing weapons that can annihilate every man, woman, and child on the planet. We can now extinguish our own species.

However, the simplest form of human behavior has eluded us. We have not learned how to get along with one another and, like our man-ape ancestors, reach for a stone or a club to settle a dispute. Our brain has evolved to become the most highly sophisticated mechanism in the known universe, and we all have one. It has solved the riddle of the atom, which is one of the greatest mysteries in nature; surely then, it can teach us the path to peace if we truly have the desire to pursue it.

# INDEX

Made in the USA
San Bernardino, CA
08 December 2014